WARBIRDTECH
SERIES

VOLUME 7

W9-BPO-128

BOEING
B-17 FLYING FORTRESS

By Frederick A. Johnsen

specialtypress
PUBLISHERS AND WHOLESALERS

Published by
Specialty Press Publishers and Wholesalers
11481 Kost Dam Road
North Branch, MN 55056
United States of America
(612) 583-3239

Distributed in the UK and Europe by
Airlife Publishing Ltd.
101 Longden Road
Shrewsbury
SY3 9EB
England

ISBN 0-933424-70-1

Material contained in this book is intended for historical and
entertainment value only, and is not to be construed as usable
for aircraft or component restoration, maintenance or use.

Designed by Greg Compton

Printed in the United States of America

TABLE OF CONTENTS 814010

THE BOEING B-17 FLYING FORTRESS

PREFACE **4**

THANKS FOR MAKING IT ALL POSSIBLE

CHAPTER 1: DESIGN OF THE FLYING FORTRESS **5**

LOFTY GOALS ON A SOLID FOUNDATION

CHAPTER 2: FIRST TO FIGHT **34**

BRITISH TRAINED IN FORTRESSES IN THE U.S.A.

CHAPTER 3: IN HARM'S WAY **36**

FLYING FORTRESSES IN COMBAT

CHAPTER 4: TESTS AND PROPOSALS **62**

EVALUATING WAYS TO IMPROVE THE B-17

SPECIAL FULL COLOR SECTION: B-17 WARPAINT **65**

THE FLYING FORTRESS IN LIVING COLOR

CHAPTER 5: POSTWAR FORTRESSES **92**

AN OLD, BUT EXPENDABLE, FRIEND

SIGNIFICANT DATES **100**

KEY DATES IN THE HISTORY OF THE B-17 FLYING FORTRESS

PREFACE

THANKS FOR MAKING IT ALL POSSIBLE

Just as actors profess a desire to play Hamlet, many aviation historians jump at the chance to write about the Boeing B-17 Flying Fortress. Everybody likes a winner, and my long-term study of B-24 Liberators notwithstanding, I too, harbor a certain reverence for the bomber that put Boeing — and Seattle — on the map, and gave its crews a much-loved vehicle in war and peace.

The B-17 ushered in a new era of bombardment aviation; its use of four engines to produce great range and speed were awesome in the 1930s. The B-17 harbored other attributes that became increasingly archaic: Tailwheel stance, split flaps, and aging airfoil being most apparent. Its construction life spanned a decade between 1935 and the end of World War Two, and its appearance went from a jazzy art deco countenance in the 1930s to a pugnacious, gun-studded warrior in the 1940s.

After the war, stripped and lightened B-17s continued to serve the modern U.S. Air Force as general-officer transports, drones, and drone directors; the Navy and Coast Guard likewise appreciated the gentle giant the Flying Fortress could be. When suppression of fire ants became a priority in the southeastern United States in the early 1960s, B-17s equipped to dispense poison were mustered for the cause.

The last hurrah for working Fortresses took place over the forests and wild lands of the U.S.A., into the 1980s, as B-17s salvoed thousands of gallons of fire retardant on seething fire lines.

Since Clark Gable boarded a B-17 in the 1930s, the Fortress has been Hollywood's bomber; the adoration continues with films that both foster and rely on public recognition of the Flying Fortress.

I was given a wonderful opportunity to learn about the B-17, and historical aviation research, when still in my teens in Seattle in the late 1960s. That was when then-director of Boeing Historical Services, the late Harl V. Brackin, Jr., and Boeing editor and historian Peter M. Bowers fostered my sometimes-brash efforts to become an aviation historian in my own right. This book is respectfully dedicated to Brackin and Bowers. Hopefully I still apply what you taught me so many years ago.

Many people have expanded my B-17 research over the years. With apologies to anyone inadvertently overlooked, I acknowledge Boeing (and Tom Cole), the Confederate Air Force, Harry Fisher, Don Hayes, Marty Isham, Don Keller (Air Depot), Arnold Kolb (Black Hills Aviation), Art Lacey, Al Lloyd, McChord Air Museum (Ed Baker and Herb Mellor) Dave Menard, L.M. Myers, Col. Tracy Petersen, USAF (Ret), Revell-Monogram Models, San Diego Aerospace Museum (especially Ray Wagner and Ron Bulinski), Carl Scholl and Tony Ritzman (Aero Trader) Bob, Dave, and Jeff Sturges

(Columbia Airmotive), and the University of Washington Aeronautical Laboratory (and Prof. William H. Rae, Jr.).

A special word is in order regarding Bob Sturges and Don Keller. Bob, as a Boeing tech rep in England during World War Two, learned more about what made the B-17 tick than probably anyone else on the planet. He parlayed this wartime expertise into a long-lived airplane parts business that specialized in B-17s for decades after the war. Always agreeable to sharing his knowledge, Bob took a liking to Don Keller and me when we were still teenagers in the era of televised episodes of *Twelve O'Clock High*. Don Keller has since gone on to operate Air Depot, a warbird memorabilia and historical parts mail-order company that also specializes in the B-17. Sturges and Keller, covering two generations, are the two best character-references the Flying Fortress could ever have.

And most certainly, the thousands of men and women who built, flew, and maintained B-17s deserve thanks. Even as this volume praises, and occasionally finds fault with, the B-17, let no one find fault with the human element — the men and women who worked marvels of production, and performed daily acts of heroism in the skies in their trusty B-17s.

FREDERICK A. JOHNSEN
1997

DESIGN OF THE FLYING FORTRESS

The engineers of the Boeing company in Seattle have a workman-like knack for adapting new technologies, and interpreting specifications with foresight and imagination, and quietly coming up with trend-setting aircraft. When Boeing's original Model 40 mailplane, with wooden fuselage and aging Liberty engine, failed to win a Post Office mailplane contract in 1925, the design languished for about a year. Boeing designers resurrected the Model 40 with a welded steel tube fuselage and a brand-new radial Pratt & Whitney Wasp powerplant. With this amalgamation of technologies, the Boeing Air Transport company was able to bid with confidence on an airmail route with the new Model 40. Its lightweight radial engine saved enough on the scales to allow for incorporation of a small cabin in the fuselage for two passengers.[1] Modest by today's standards, the Model 40 was right on the money for 1927,

and set airmail standards until superseded by another Boeing design that embraced technology — the all-metal, cantilever-wing monoplane Model 247 of 1933.

With the 247, Boeing had evolved a style and design rationale that would endure for more than a decade. A wing of broad chord, designed with bridge-like rib trusses and built-up spars, owed much to Boeing's earlier pioneering cantilever designs including the single-engine Monomail and twin engine B-9 bomber. The Boeing 247 airliner was a technical and financial success for the Boeing company, although its dominion of the com-

mercial airways was soon challenged by the Douglas DC-series.

With characteristic economy, Boeing engineers turned their talents toward devising a new bomber for the Air Corps in 1934, using many of the construction methods they had already verified in the 247 and B-9, and adding an interpretive twist when it came to powerplants. The Air Corps call for bomber proposals in 1934 specified multi-engine. Boeing's competitors, including Douglas with its B-18 of obvious DC airliner genesis, all relied on two engines. Existing four-engine designs tended to burden the engines with the largest

The original Boeing Model 299 prototype of the Flying Fortress series was manually positioned on the ramp in front of a brick Boeing hangar in Seattle in 1935. Unlike production Fortresses, landing gear struts on the prototype straddled the mainwheels. (Mrs. Stephen McElroy)

(Left) As photographed on a B-17B in February 1940, the redesigned B-17 main landing gear featured braces ahead of a single forward-retracting main strut. (Boeing via Peter M. Bowers)

Three service-test Y1B-17s flew what was captioned as the "first Flying Fortress formation in echelon" on 12 May 1937. Teardrop waist, ventral, and dorsal gun blisters were superseded by more effective gun positions as Fortress design evolved. Recessed bombardier's station is evident by kinked look to the chin of Fortresses prior to the B-17B. (Mrs. Stephen McElroy)

airframe and weight possible, invariably degrading performance. Boeing's bold proposal for the new bomber competition was to use four engines, while observing the design discipline to produce a smaller airframe than other four-engine aircraft of the day, resulting in a bomber with impressive performance instead of ponderous flight traits.

The trim Boeing four-engine bomber had a wingspan only slightly more than eight feet greater than that of the twin-engine Douglas competitor. Given Boeing model number 299, the new bomber was in design by the summer of 1934, with construction beginning that August. First flight of the original 299 was 28 July 1935. Less than a month later, it was flown to Wright Field for evaluations. It was quickly obvious the new Boeing outperformed its competition. But contract selection was not so simple. A lingering inertia in Congress favored the more traditional twin-engine designs; those who argued in favor of the Douglas twin said more bombers could be bought for the same amount of money.

Y1B-17 of the 96th Bombardment Squadron showed attempts to streamline the landing gear with fairings not found on later wartime production variants. (Peter M. Bowers collection)

Its full potential still not totally explored, the Model 299 crashed at Wright Field on 30 October 1935 on takeoff, with the control locks inadvertently engaged. Much as the crash of the new XP-38 Lightning several years later did not kill that promising program, so did the Flying Fortress outlive the demise of the prototype. Gen. H.H. Arnold and other Air Corps visionaries were singular in their view of the future of long-range strategic bombardment, and they nurtured the Flying Fortress for that role. Funds were forthcoming to build 13 service-test Fortresses, similar to the original Model 299. Contracted as YB-17, and then redesignated Y1B-17 to clarify a funding source, these aircraft ultimately became designated B-17, with no prefixes or suffixes, upon completion of their service test period. Salient contribution of the Y1B-17 to the Fortress formula was replacement of the 299's Pratt and Whitney Hornet engines with Wright SGR-1820-39 Cyclones. From that point on, combat B-17s would fly with Wright R-1820 Cyclones of varying models. Fine-tuning of armament and landing gear was made on the Y1B-17s, and crew complement was set at six, two less than in the original 299. First flight of a Y1B-17 was 2 December 1936.[2]

Disaster was averted aboard a Y1B-17 (36-157) when its robust structure survived flight in a severe storm. The Air Corps used this experience to validate the strength of the airframe, and released an additional static test airframe to be completed by Boeing as an additional flying example. Designated Y1B-17A, this aircraft first flew on 29 April 1938, and ultimately contributed the use of turbosuperchargers on subsequent Fortresses.

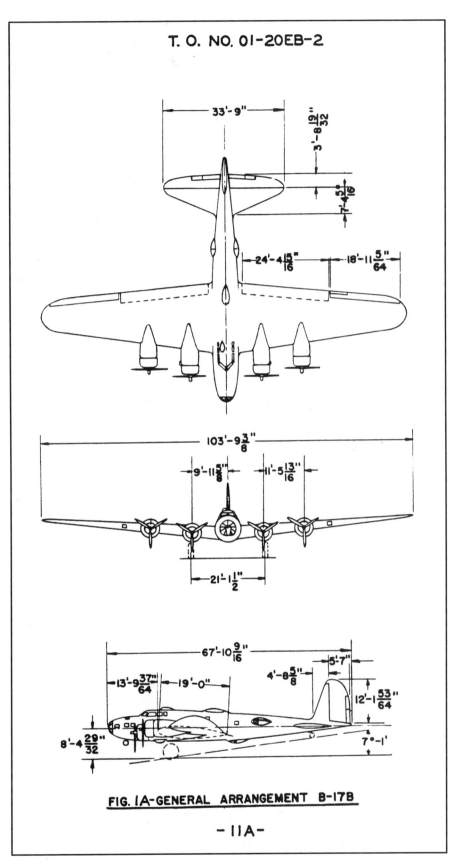

T. O. NO. 01-20EB-2

FIG. IA-GENERAL ARRANGEMENT B-17B

- IIA -

B-17B general arrangement drawing from a pre-war erection and maintenance manual shows pertinent dimensions. (Don Keller/Columbia Airmotive)

Washable camouflage was tried on a host of Air Corps aircraft including this Y1B-17; the paint obliterated even national insignia. (Peter M. Bowers collection)

Now the Wright Cyclones had the altitude boost they needed for the B-17's intended mission.

The B-17B represented the first true production model of the Flying Fortress. The B-model introduced the flattened, multi-ribbed nosepiece that remained essentially unchanged through production of the B-17E. B-models also used a larger rudder than previous Fortresses, and bigger flaps. Pneumatic brakes were replaced by hydraulic ones on the B-17B.

B-17Cs did away with the remaining teardrop gun blisters on the sides and belly of the Fortress, using flush elliptical waist windows and a larger "bathtub" ventral gun

Originally purchased by the Air Corps for destruction on the ground to verify the structure's limits, this airframe was finished for flight as the sole Y1B-17A in 1938. It contributed to the effectiveness of the Fortress by serving as a testbed for turbosupercharger installations, seen in the photo on top of the nacelles. Ultimately, the turbosuperchargers were mounted into the bottom surfaces of the nacelles on production models. (Peter M. Bowers collection)

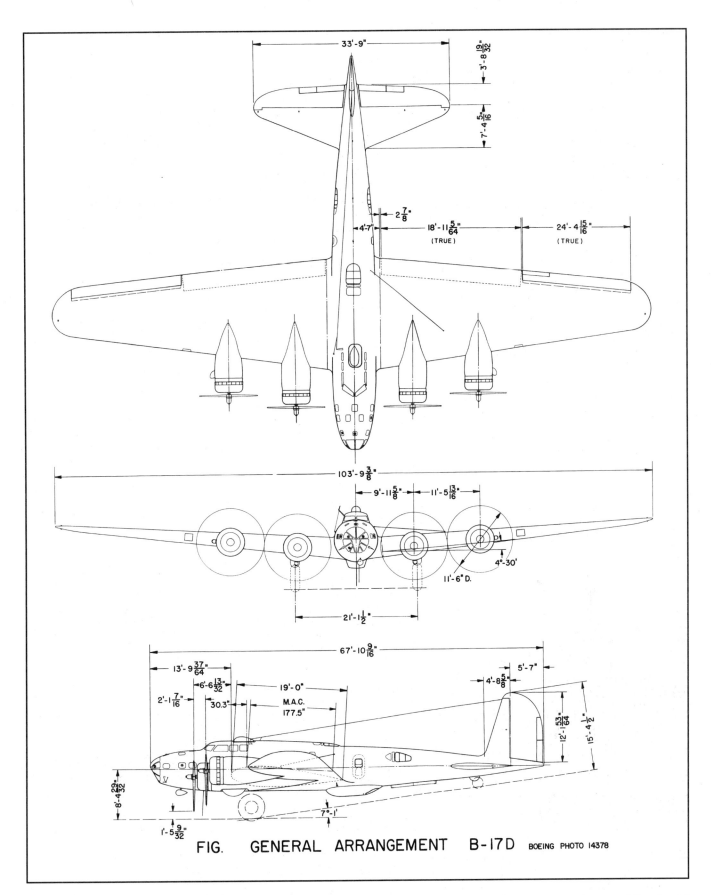

FIG. GENERAL ARRANGEMENT B-17D BOEING PHOTO 14378

B-17D three-view shows design evolution, including basic radio room hatch configuration and ventral "bathtub" gun emplacement introduced on C-model. (Boeing via Peter M. Bowers)

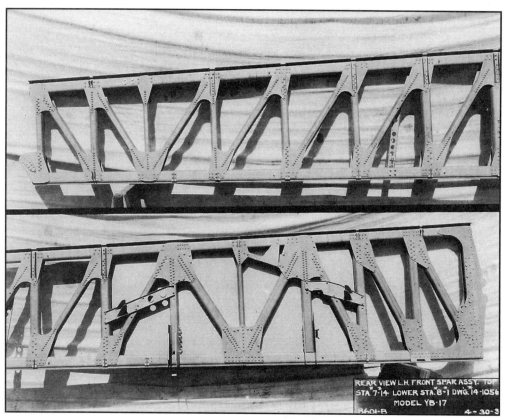

REAR VIEW L.H. FRONT SPAR ASSY. TOP
STA. 7·14 LOWER STA.8·1 DWG. 14·1056
MODEL YB·17
B601·B   4·30·3

Legendary bridge-like built-up wing spars of the B-17 inspired confidence in the design. Photo of YB-17 spar assemblies was taken the last day of April 1936. (Boeing via Peter M. Bowers)

emplacement. The radio compartment gun window also nested closer to the fuselage beginning with the C-model. Self-sealing fuel tanks and crew position armor plating made the B-17C more combat-worthy. The first flight of a B-17C was 21 July 1940. Thirty-eight were built before production shifted to the very similar B-17D,

INBD. WING SECTION READY FOR INST B-17B 11845-B 9-7-39

View into the wing of a B-17B from the fuselage joint shows zig-zag bracing. (Peter M. Bowers collection)

WARBIRD**TECH**
S E R I E S

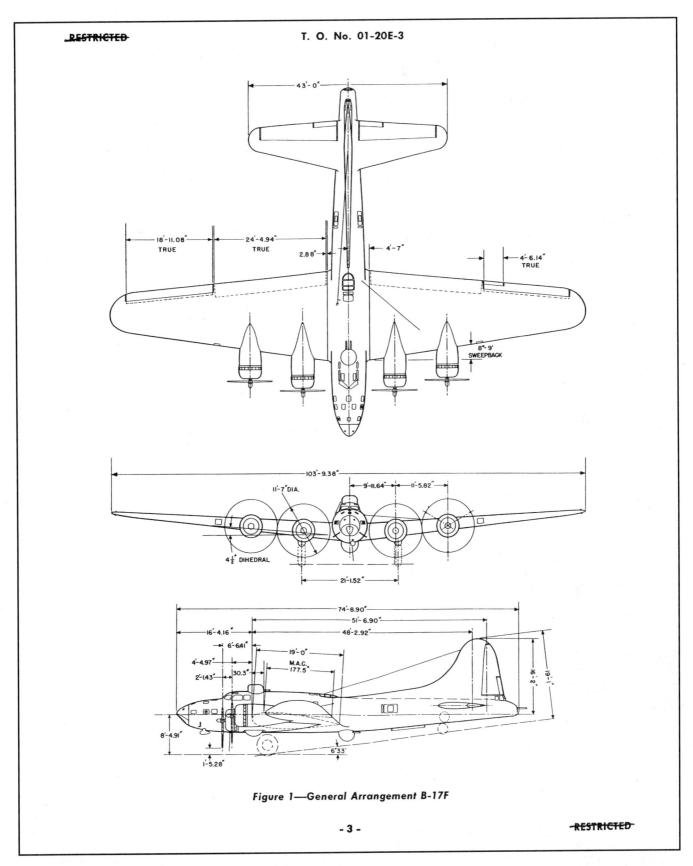

Figure 1—General Arrangement B-17F

Three-view B-17F drawing from the structural repair manual shows relocation of the front windscreen closer to the nose than on the D-model, a change that began with the heavily redesigned B-17E. Changes in horizontal tail configuration incorporated in E-models is also evident. (Carl Scholl/Aero Trader)

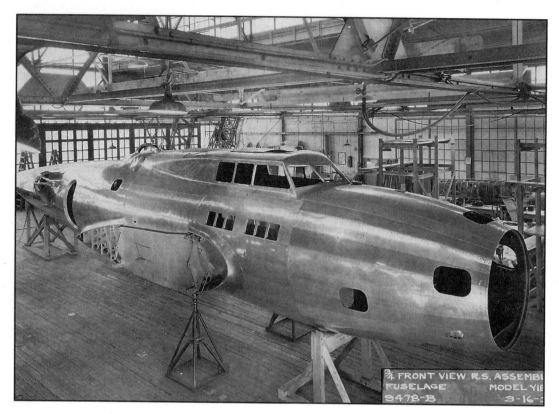

In an elegantly simple Boeing shop in March 1937, a Y1B-17 fuselage took form on wooden stands and jacks — a far cry from the relentless pace of wartime Fortress production that ensued. Even as basic fuselage form remained recognizable throughout production, placement of windows in nose and location and shape of rear crew entry door changed significantly. (Peter M. Bowers collection)

chiefly distinguishable for its addition of cowl flaps which became standard on subsequent B-17s. An additional crew member was carried on the D-models.

Major revision to the tail of the B-17E gave the Flying Fortress its signature appearance with a sweeping dorsal fin mounting a revised rudder, beneath which, for the first time in a B-17, a tail gun emplacement was provided by the factory. First flight of the B-17E was 5 September 1941. Planform of the horizontal stabilizers and elevators also changed at this time. The E-model also introduced a Sperry

Around 1938 the Golden Gate Exposition at San Francisco included a Y1B-17 that was seen some of the time in natural metal finish, and some of the time in variegated camouflage. The B-17 was part of a deliberate publicity campaign by the Air Corps intended to promote its value to the nation. (Carl and Helen Johnsen)

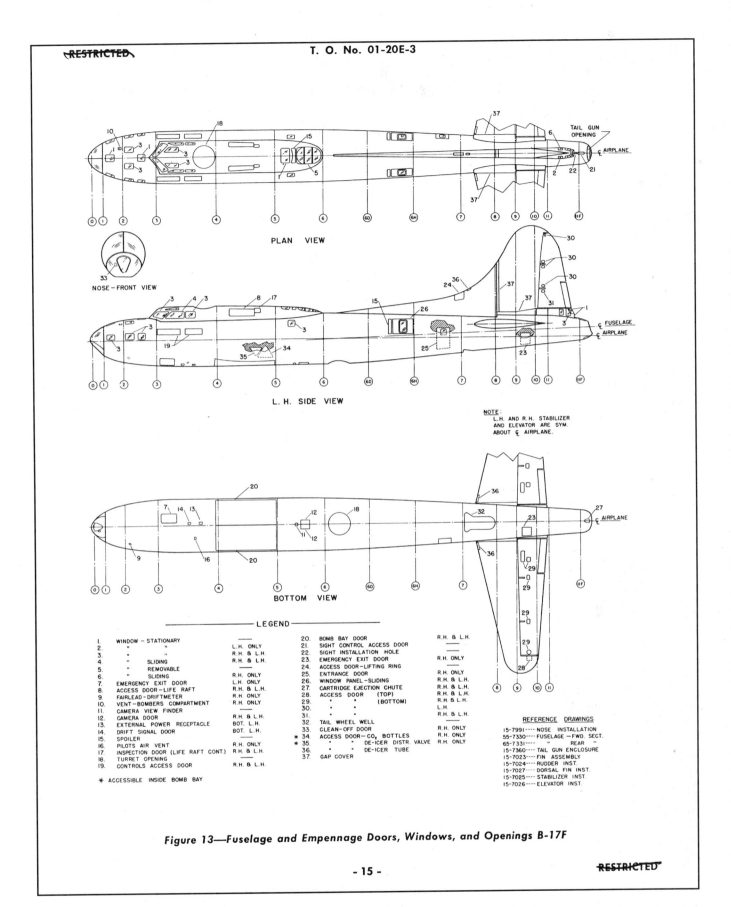

PLAN VIEW

NOSE — FRONT VIEW

L. H. SIDE VIEW

NOTE:
L.H. AND R.H. STABILIZER
AND ELEVATOR ARE SYM.
ABOUT ₵ AIRPLANE.

BOTTOM VIEW

— LEGEND —

1.	WINDOW – STATIONARY	—
2.	" "	L.H. ONLY
3.	" "	R.H. & L.H.
4.	" SLIDING	R.H. & L.H.
5.	" REMOVABLE	—
6.	" SLIDING	R.H. ONLY
7.	EMERGENCY EXIT DOOR	L.H. ONLY
8.	ACCESS DOOR – LIFE RAFT	R.H. & L.H.
9.	FAIRLEAD – DRIFTMETER	R.H. ONLY
10.	VENT – BOMBERS COMPARTMENT	R.H. ONLY
11.	CAMERA VIEW FINDER	—
12.	CAMERA DOOR	R.H. & L.H.
13.	EXTERNAL POWER RECEPTACLE	BOT. L.H.
14.	DRIFT SIGNAL DOOR	BOT. L.H.
15.	SPOILER	—
16.	PILOTS AIR VENT	R.H. ONLY
17.	INSPECTION DOOR (LIFE RAFT CONT.)	R.H. & L.H.
18.	TURRET OPENING	—
19.	CONTROLS ACCESS DOOR	R.H. & L.H.

20.	BOMB BAY DOOR	R.H. & L.H.
21.	SIGHT CONTROL ACCESS DOOR	—
22.	SIGHT INSTALLATION HOLE	—
23.	EMERGENCY EXIT DOOR	R.H. ONLY
24.	ACCESS DOOR – LIFTING RING	—
25.	ENTRANCE DOOR	R.H. ONLY
26.	WINDOW PANEL – SLIDING	R.H. & L.H.
27.	CARTRIDGE EJECTION CHUTE	R.H. & L.H.
28.	ACCESS DOOR (TOP)	R.H. & L.H.
29.	" " (BOTTOM)	R.H. & L.H.
30.	" "	L.H.
31.	" "	R.H. & L.H.
32.	TAIL WHEEL WELL	
33.	CLEAN-OFF DOOR	
✳ 34.	ACCESS DOOR – CO_2 BOTTLES	R.H. ONLY
✳ 35.	" " DE-ICER DISTR. VALVE	R.H. ONLY
36.	" " DE-ICER TUBE	
37.	GAP COVER	

✳ ACCESSIBLE INSIDE BOMB BAY

REFERENCE DRAWINGS

15-7991 ---- NOSE INSTALLATION
55-7330 ---- FUSELAGE — FWD. SECT.
65-7331 ---- " REAR "
15-7360 ---- TAIL GUN ENCLOSURE
15-7023 ---- FIN ASSEMBLY
15-7024 ---- RUDDER INST.
15-7027 ---- DORSAL FIN INST.
15-7025 ---- STABILIZER INST.
15-7026 ---- ELEVATOR INST.

Figure 13—Fuselage and Empennage Doors, Windows, and Openings B-17F

- 15 -

Tech order drawing depicting openings in a B-17F reveals slight asymmetry to tailwheel well. Camera doors (item 12) afforded ball turret gunner an opportunity to clean the sighting window of his turret in flight. (Carl Scholl/Aero Trader)

BOEING
B-17 FLYING FORTRESS

A Y1B-17 in flight shows the Wright Field arrow logo. Lack of anti-glare panel ahead of windscreen would be rectified. (SDAM)

power turret on top of the fuse-lage aft of the cockpit, and, on the first 112 B-17Es, a remotely-sighted belly power turret, each mounting two .50-caliber machine guns, as did the tail position.[3]

Development of uniquely American power turrets, mounting twin .50-caliber machine guns, apparently was largely an independent venture, as Great Britain's Air Ministry guarded information about its own power turret developments in 1940, when U.S. Air Corps observers went to England. British skeptics noted America's neutrality at that time, and wondered if British military secrets might wind up in the hands of Britain's enemies. Ultimately, the American air attaches to Great Britain were not to be shown detailed drawings of British power turrets. One of the first American attaches to arrive in April 1940 was Lt. Col. Grandison Gardner, whose background in armaments no doubt expedited his desire to see America incorporate British power gun turrets,

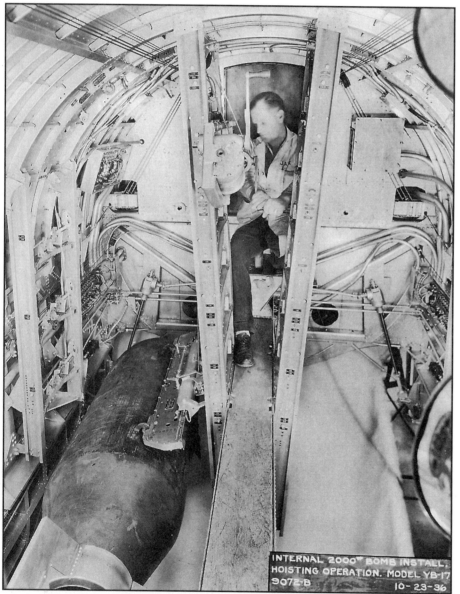

INTERNAL 2000" BOMB INSTALL. HOISTING OPERATION. MODEL YB-17 9072-B   10-23-36

A 2,000-pound bomb was a snug fit in the bay of a YB-17 in 1936. Angled inboard bomb racks provided slim passageway through bomb bay. Upon first entering a B-17, visitors frequently remark how small it is, as evidenced by this catwalk through the bomb bay. The size was in keeping with Boeing's design rationale to use four engines to boost performance, not to heft the biggest possible airframe. (Peter M. Bowers collection)

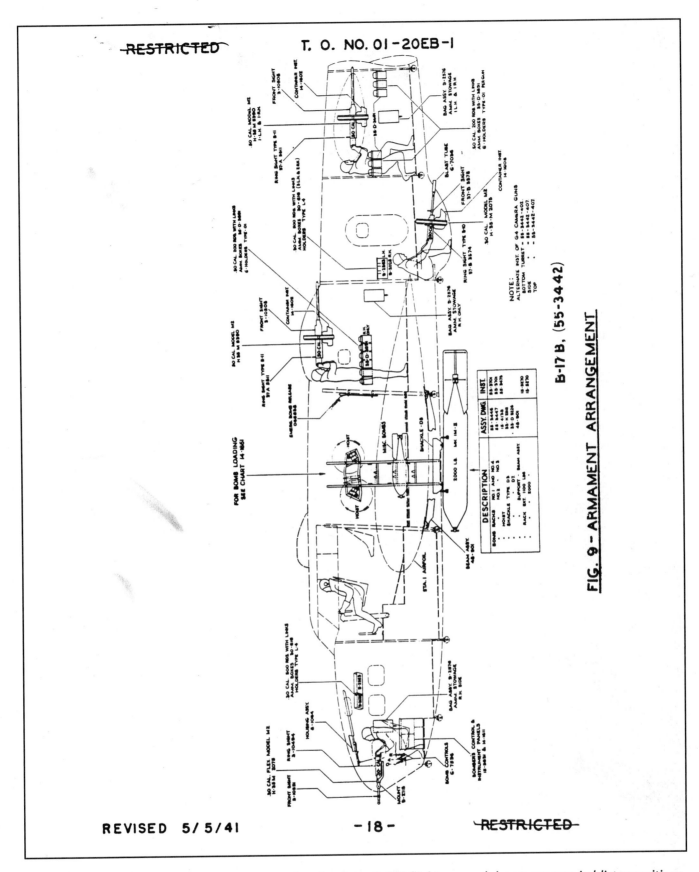

Depicting pre-war style of bombs, armament drawing from B-17B flight manual shows gunners in blister positions. Galvanized type O-1 ammunition cans are shown stowed near the waist and radio compartment .50-caliber guns; ventral armament is .30-caliber. (Don Keller collection)

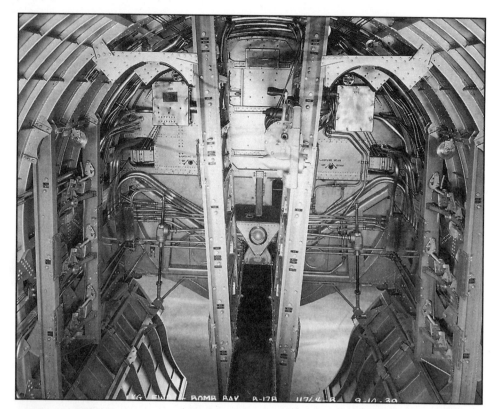

B-17B shows characteristic bomb bay door ribs and jack screws for opening and closing. (Peter M. Bowers collection)

or, if those designs would not be made available, American originals should be created.[4] (This may in part explain why the first versions of the Liberator to carry a British power turret, the British Liberator IIs, were sent from the U.S. with no turrets in place, the units being installed after the Liberator IIs arrived in Great Britain. Ultimately, American power turrets were produced and in service in late 1941 on B-17Es and early 1942 on Liberators. In an ironic twist, American Martin top turrets even found their way onto some British-designed Avro Lancaster heavy bombers built in Canada during the war.)

Beginning with the 113th B-17E, the remote lower turret was replaced with the Sperry-designed lower ball turret, encapsulating a gunner and his two .50-

B-17B fuselage framework in progress in January 1939 shows cutout in top of fuselage for cockpit cabin superstructure; aft of cockpit, the superstructure was a fairing applied on top of circular fuselage members. (Peter M. Bowers collection)

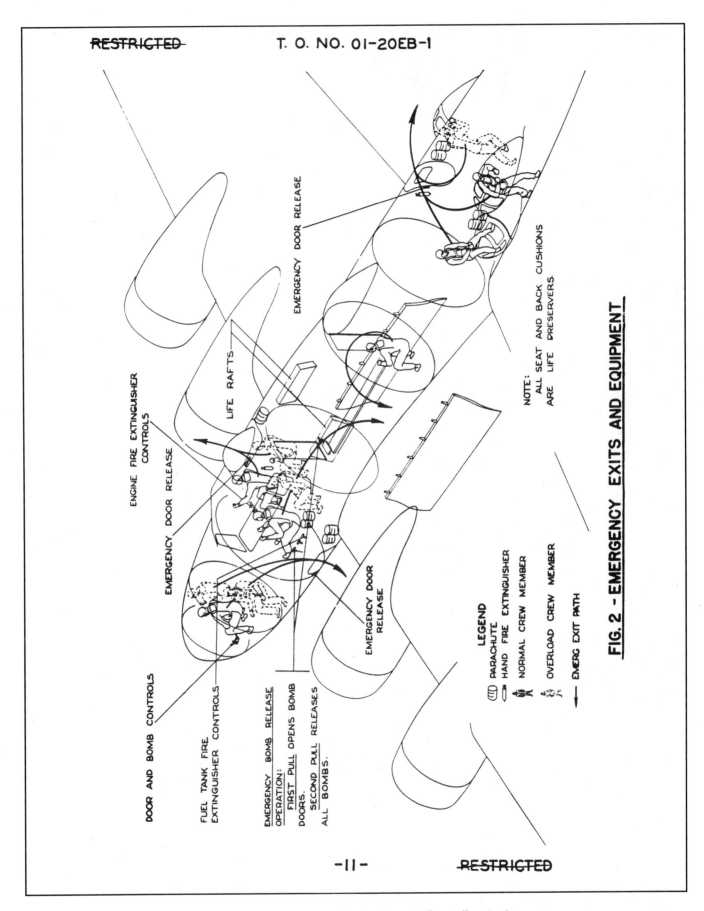

FIG. 2 - EMERGENCY EXITS AND EQUIPMENT

EMERGENCY DOOR RELEASE

NOTE:
ALL SEAT AND BACK CUSHIONS
ARE LIFE PRESERVERS.

ENGINE FIRE EXTINGUISHER CONTROLS

LIFE RAFTS

EMERGENCY DOOR RELEASE

DOOR AND BOMB CONTROLS

FUEL TANK FIRE EXTINGUISHER CONTROLS

EMERGENCY BOMB RELEASE
OPERATION:
FIRST PULL OPENS BOMB DOORS.
SECOND PULL RELEASES ALL BOMBS.

EMERGENCY DOOR RELEASE

LEGEND
PARACHUTE
HAND FIRE EXTINGUISHER
NORMAL CREW MEMBER
OVERLOAD CREW MEMBER
EMERG EXIT PATH

B-17B flight manual drawing shows crew positions and exits. (Don Keller collection)

BOEING
B-17 FLYING FORTRESS

caliber weapons. The B-17E was the first USAAF Fortress to enter combat over Europe, although B-17Cs given to the British as Fortress Is saw combat earlier.

The B-17F is at first distinguishable from later E-models by the F's use of a longer Plexiglas nose piece with no metal ribbing. F-models were also fitted with wider paddle-blade propellers for altitude performance, and, as with the B-24, this change necessitated a revision to the engine cowling to permit the wider blades to feather. Self-sealing oil tanks were added to the F-model, and so-called Tokyo tanks added 1,100 additional gallons of gas to the capacity of later B-17Fs by filling space in the wings. B-17Fs typically employed enlarged and staggered cheek gun windows.[5]

Bombardier's station on a B-17B in September 1939 was clean, simple, and almost airliner-like compared to its later combat siblings. Double handles above far corner of seat cushion are bomb release levers. (Peter M. Bowers collection)

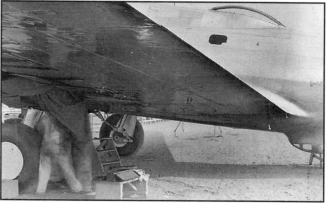

Split flap is seen extended and closed on a B-17B in 1939. That same year, Consolidated used more sophisticated and effective Fowler area-increasing flaps on its B-24; Boeing followed suit with Fowler flaps on the B-29. (Peter M. Bowers collection)

(Opposite page) Drawing from the B-17G illustrated parts book shows Plexiglas nose basically as introduced on F-model (top drawing) and later configuration produced during G-series production. When used on early G-models, the older nose deleted dimples and sockets for flexible machine gun mounts as had been installed on F-models. Knockout window for cleaning bombsight glass was elongated on old nose, and circular on G-specific variants. Bombsight windows, made of sandwiched safety glass which was optically superior to Plexiglas, also changed dimensions for these two nose styles. A sub-variation among late B-17G noses occurred, with some having a uniformly curved upper portion, possibly to accommodate optics of compensating gunsights like the K-13 for the chin turret. Nose pieces could be interchanged between B-17Es, Fs, and Gs, as the basic adjoining fuselage structure remained the same. (Carl Scholl/Aero Trader)

FUSELAGE

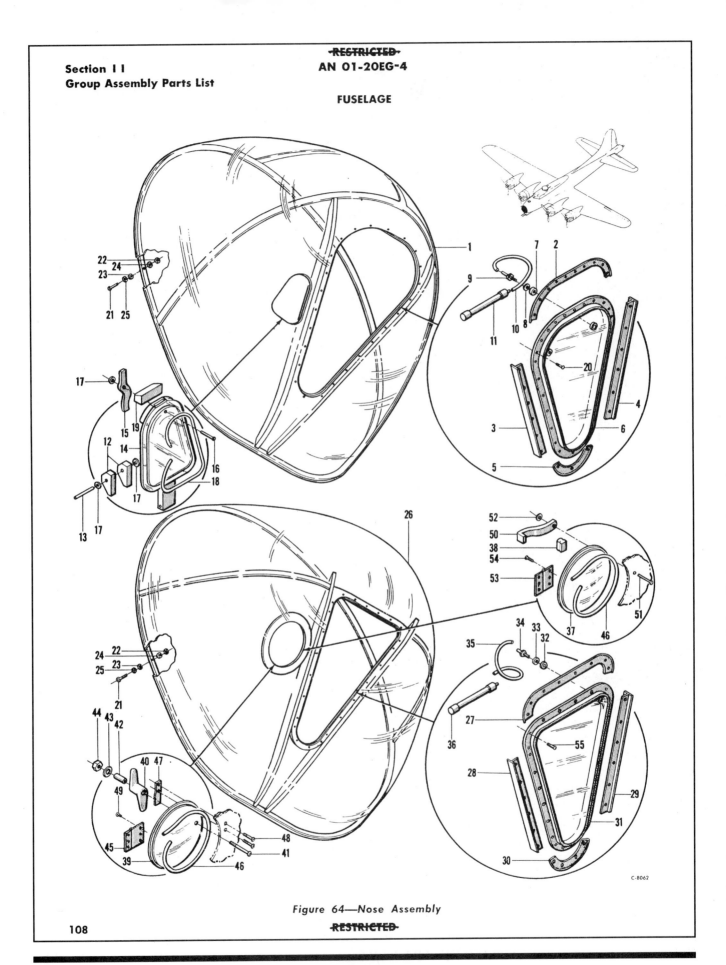

Figure 64—Nose Assembly

BOEING
B-17 FLYING FORTRESS

The pre-war B-17B could be fitted with bench seat berths in the waist section. Control cables were routed openly overhead. (Boeing via Peter M. Bowers collection)

Last production revision to the Fortress line was the B-17G, distinctive for its use of a Bendix remotely-sighted chin turret to deter frontal attacks. A turret of this type had been tried on the YB-40 escort variant of the Fortress, and found favor even while the rest of the sluggish YB-40 was quickly dismissed as unsuitable. Later, B-17Gs used staggered waist windows to afford more room to the gunners. After producing the B-17G with no cheek guns because of the availability of the chin turret, cheek guns were re-introduced. Staggered and slightly raised cheek gun windows on G-models typically were the opposite stagger of that employed on F-models, although the occasional F-model was photographed with staggered cheek windows approximating the G-

Closely-cowled Wright R-1820 engine on a B-17B was revealed with cowlings removed in the Boeing plant in the summer of 1939. Feathering Hamilton-Standard three-blade propellers were used. (Peter M. Bowers collection)

FUSELAGE

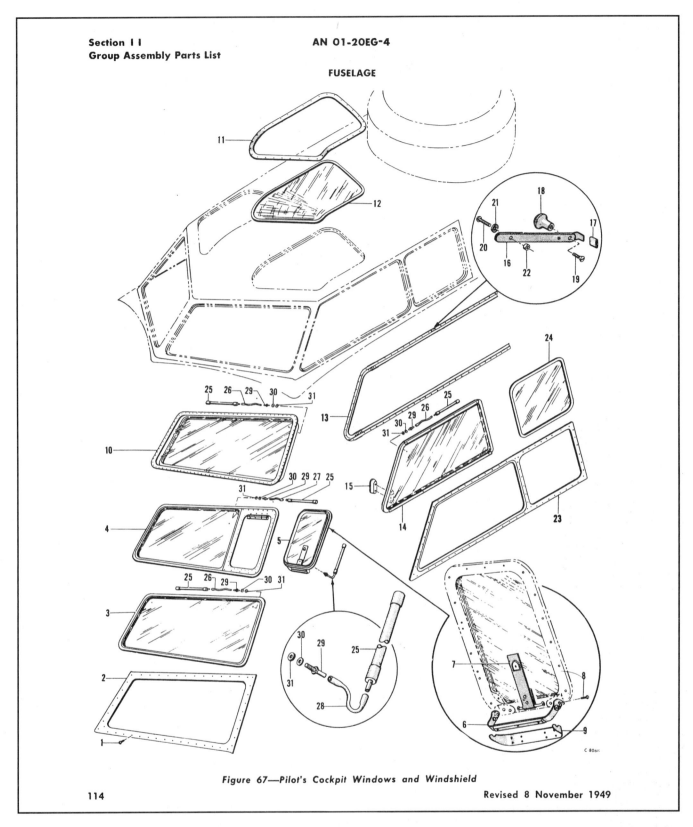

Figure 67—Pilot's Cockpit Windows and Windshield

Cockpit glazing for B-17Gs could include thick, heavy, bullet-resistant windscreen panels (part 10 in the photo), or two-part thin safety glass with an opening clear-view knockout window that hinged up and in (part 4), or a light safety glass panel with an airspace between panes (part 3). Some sliding side windows had metal reinforced handles in the lower front corner; others relied on a clear glass handle glued to the inside corner of the window glass. (Carl Scholl/Aero Trader)

B-17B number 38-221, photographed with number one propeller feathered, was operated by the 32nd Bombardment Squadron. (Boardman C. Reed via SDAM)

B-17C at Boeing Field showed new bathtub ventral gun emplacement instead of teardrop blister there. Photo taken in the late summer of 1940. (SDAM)

configuration. Even the tail stinger underwent transformation during production of B-17Gs, with some aircraft using the earlier factory-style tail gun emplacement while later aircraft had the Cheyenne tail gun fixture which provided a greater field of fire and had a revised bulbous metal shroud for the guns and a curved Plexiglas enclosure for the gunner, with flat armor glass mounted inside.

A dozen B-17Gs modified to carry lifeboats for search

Black drift sight extends beneath the forward compartment of a B-17B photographed in August 1939. Large circular loop antenna for direction-finding gear was offset under the nose; later versions would be housed in a teardrop streamlined fairing. B-model introduced "birdcage" nose retained through production of the B-17E. (Boeing via SDAM)

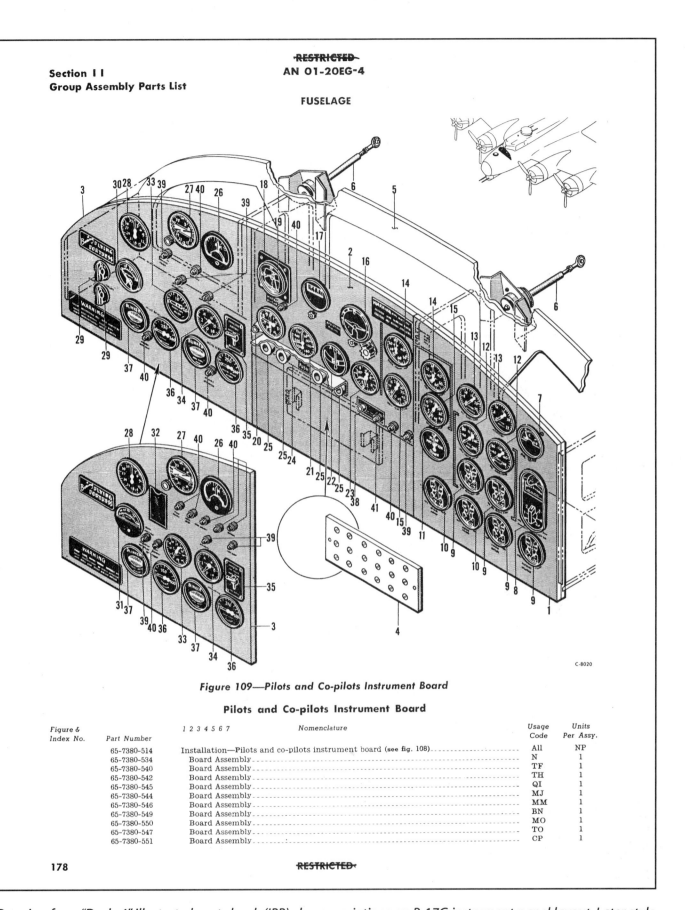

Figure 109—Pilots and Co-pilots Instrument Board

Pilots and Co-pilots Instrument Board

Figure & Index No.	Part Number	1 2 3 4 5 6 7 Nomenclature	Usage Code	Units Per Assy.
	65-7380-514	Installation—Pilots and co-pilots instrument board (see fig. 108)	All	NP
	65-7380-534	Board Assembly	N	1
	65-7380-540	Board Assembly	TF	1
	65-7380-542	Board Assembly	TH	1
	65-7380-545	Board Assembly	QI	1
	65-7380-544	Board Assembly	MJ	1
	65-7380-546	Board Assembly	MM	1
	65-7380-549	Board Assembly	BN	1
	65-7380-550	Board Assembly	MO	1
	65-7380-547	Board Assembly	TO	1
	65-7380-551	Board Assembly	CP	1

Drawing from "Dash-4" illustrated parts book (IPB) shows variations on B-17G instrument panel layout. Later style Boeing Flying Fortress nameplate is represented on left panel. (Carl Scholl/Aero Trader)

BOEING
B-17 FLYING FORTRESS

"Bathtub" belly gun on a B-17C, fitted with a single .50-caliber machine gun. Extendable wind deflector helped block slipstream. Later ball turret with 360-degree azimuth was far better solution for ventral protection. When not in use, this ventral gun position was covered with a hinged panel inside the fuselage. (Boeing)

and rescue missions were redesignated B-17Hs before the nomenclature was revised to SB-17G. Other prefix and suffix letters identified modified B-17s, usually starting as G-models, used for tests and special missions after World War Two.[6]

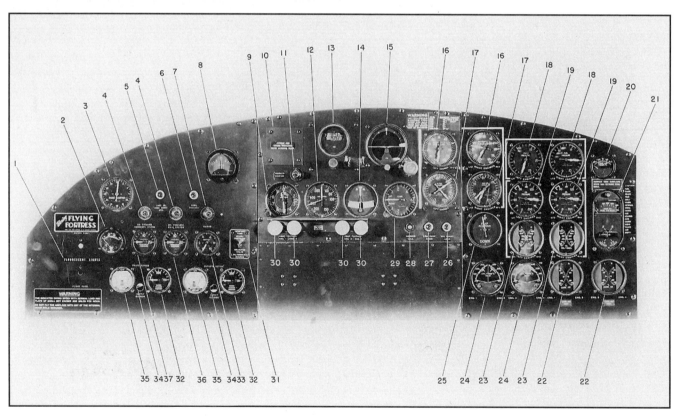

Nomenclature on the photo calls this a B-17 instrument panel (with no prefix or suffix letters). Dated 8 April 1938, this photo almost certainly depicts one of the Y1B-17s, which were called simply B-17s upon completion of service tests. Boeing totem pole logo and name Flying Fortress are affixed to the copilot's side of the instrument panel. Wood-and-metal control wheels reminiscent of the old Model 80 trimotor airliner were used into B-17E production. (Mrs. Stephen McElroy)

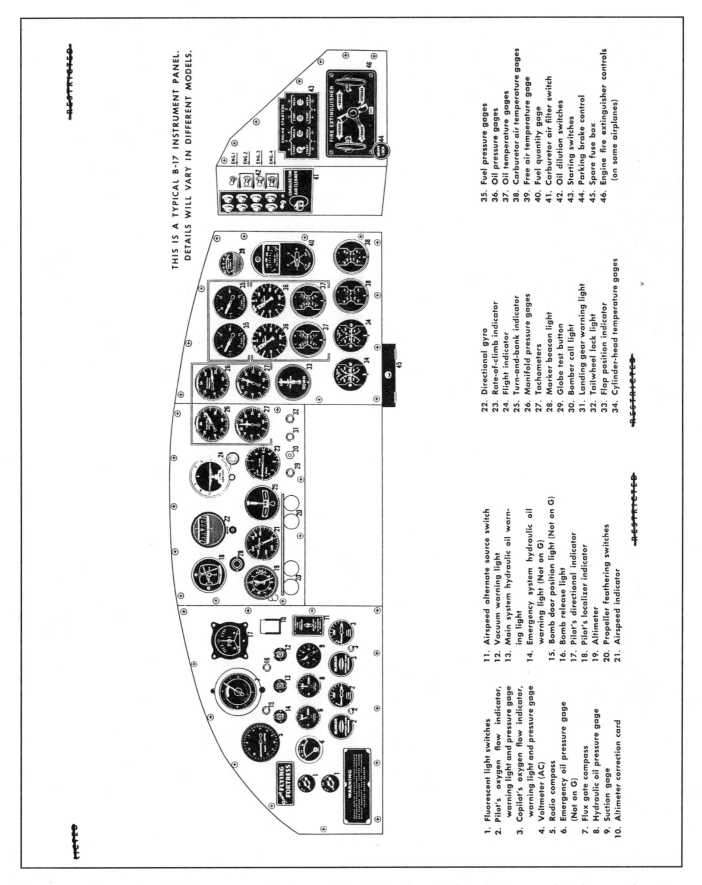

THIS IS A TYPICAL B-17 INSTRUMENT PANEL.
DETAILS WILL VARY IN DIFFERENT MODELS.

1. Fluorescent light switches
2. Pilot's oxygen flow indicator, warning light and pressure gage
3. Copilot's oxygen flow indicator, warning light and pressure gage
4. Voltmeter (AC)
5. Radio compass
6. Emergency oil pressure gage (Not on G)
7. Flux gate compass
8. Hydraulic oil pressure gage
9. Suction gage
10. Altimeter correction card

11. Airspeed alternate source switch
12. Vacuum warning light
13. Main system hydraulic oil warning light
14. Emergency system hydraulic oil warning light (Not on G)
15. Bomb door position light (Not on G)
16. Bomb release light
17. Pilot's directional indicator
18. Pilot's localizer indicator
19. Altimeter
20. Propeller feathering switches
21. Airspeed indicator

22. Directional gyro
23. Rate-of-climb indicator
24. Flight indicator
25. Turn-and-bank indicator
26. Manifold pressure gages
27. Tachometers
28. Marker beacon light
29. Globe test button
30. Bomber call light
31. Landing gear warning light
32. Tailwheel lock light
33. Flap position indicator
34. Cylinder-head temperature gages

35. Fuel pressure gages
36. Oil pressure gages
37. Oil temperature gages
38. Carburetor air temperature gages
39. Free air temperature gage
40. Fuel quantity gage
41. Carburetor air filter switch
42. Oil dilution switches
43. Starting switches
44. Parking brake control
45. Spare fuse box
46. Engine fire extinguisher controls (on some airplanes)

Representative combat B-17 instrument panel was shown in line form in the pilot's manual, with an explanatory key to the instruments. (Carl Scholl/Aero Trader)

Waist blisters on Model 299 used a slot to allow single machine gun to traverse. Bead sight on end of muzzle was fitted with weather vane to compensate for position of gun relative to slipstream and movement of the aircraft. (Boeing)

FORTS FOR THE NAVY

In 1945, the U.S. Navy obtained 48 B-17Gs as PB-1s. The Fortress was selected by the Navy to carry a belly-mounted radome for use on picket missions to protect the fleet. Experience with Japanese attackers showed surface ships used as pickets to alert the main fleet suffered an unacceptably high loss rate. Airborne warning radar could see farther than surface radar, and would probably be exposed to fewer attacks. In fact, so confident were some Navy planners that the picket aircraft would be survivable, they at one point favored using unarmed C-54 transports to mount the big APS-20E search radar. But other proponents of aerial pickets, including Cdr. Henry Rowe

Early stowed waist gun installation in a rain-speckled flush B-17B teardrop window used a rudimentary recoil adaptor similar to later oil-damped Bell E-11 mount. Ammunition can is visible to the right of the gun. To stow gun, bead sight had to be rotated to the side to clear top of the fuselage of the B-17B in this set-up. (Peter M. Bowers collection)

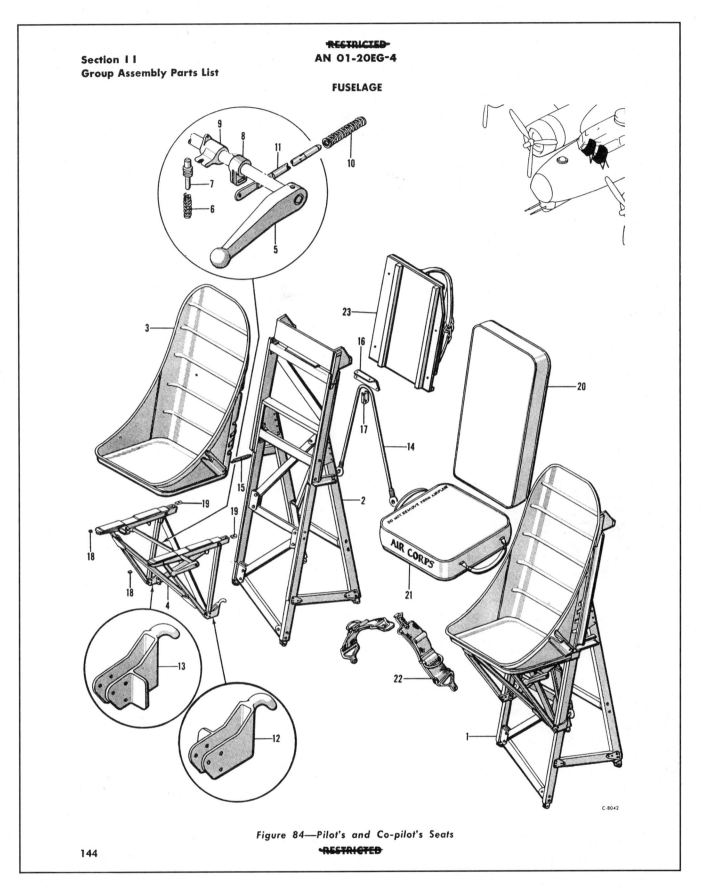

Figure 84—Pilot's and Co-pilot's Seats

Elaborate truss structure positioned B-17 pilot seats at correct height in cockpit, as seen in drawing from B-17G illustrated parts book. (Carl Scholl/Aero Trader)

who would become executive officer of the picket squadron, argued successfully that any pickets over the Sea of Japan must be armed. The B-17G became the platform of choice for armed picket duty. In training at USAAF B-17 bases, the crews of the Navy PB-1s included navigators who were taught how to fire the twin .50-caliber chin turret guns, as other crewmen learned about the other

Lefthand B-17F cheek gun required reinforced bracket to support K-4 socket in enlarged window. Dark green interior paint replaced aluminum silver in some crew areas of wartime B-17s. Bell E-11 recoil adaptor was fitted with large hoop at grips attached to supporting cable. (Boeing)

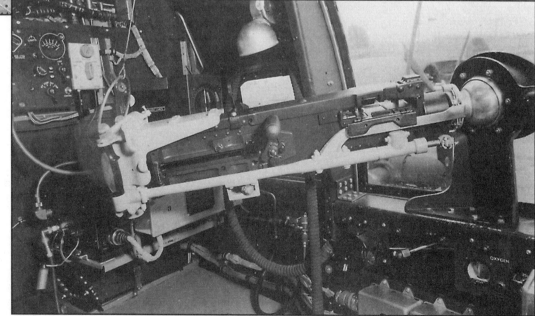

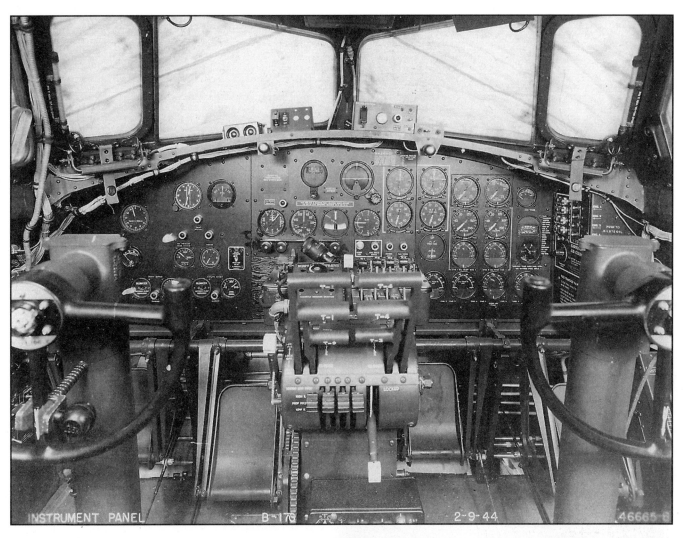

INSTRUMENT PANEL — B-17G — 2-9-44 — 46665-B

(Above) Cockpit of B-17G shows windscreen fitted with openable clear-view panels. Pilot's control yoke has aileron lock installed, clamping lower spoke of control wheel. Left rudder pedal is pushed far forward, which causes right pedal to move back, as if for an exaggerated left turn or skid. Control wheels are black-dipped castings instead of earlier wood-and-aluminum construction. Photo taken 9 February 1944. (Peter M. Bowers collection)

(Right) Shopworn early B-17E cockpit was photographed from the pilot's side. Aluminum floor has been polished by sliding feet until paint remains only around rivet heads. Throttle grips to the right of the control yoke were ingeniously designed to allow all four throttles to be manipulated simultaneously in one hand by gripping the middle set of four horizontal handles as a unit. To move any one throttle, or to move the inboard or outboard throttles in unison, the upper or lower sets of grips could be used as appropriate. (Peter M. Bowers collection)

T'S RUDDER & BRAKE PEDALS - CONTROL COL. INST B-17E 18606-

Spacious flight deck of a pre-war B-17D gave way to wartime necessities including a top power turret added in the B-17E and subsequent versions. Life raft release handles are mounted to ceiling in left rear of photo. Mission commander or additional aircrew could occupy the extra seats. Rearmost side window was deleted beginning with the revamped B-17E. (Peter M. Bowers collection)

gun emplacements in a G-model Fortress. Using the project name Cadillac II, Navy Squadron VPB-101 was equipped with the PB-1s which had belly radar pods in the bomb bay location housing eight-foot radar spinners. The picket Fortresses were given the suffix letter W, making the nomenclature PB-1W. The war ended abruptly in August 1945 before the squadron had taken delivery of its navalized Fortresses.[7]

After receiving a PB-1 without radar for familiarization in September 1945, VPB-101 did not get its first opera-

Freshly-camouflaged B-17C at March Field, California, shows Plexiglas observer's window on flight deck, and long Plexiglas tail cap. (United States Air Force)

Model configuration with extended dorsal fin introduced on the E-model was tested with powered motors to simulate prop wash in the University of Washington wind tunnel; some intermediate tail shapes reminiscent of the Boeing Sea Ranger were also modeled for the B-17 before the final configuration was chosen. (Univ. of Washington Aeronautical Laboratory photo courtesy Prof. William H. Rae, Jr.)

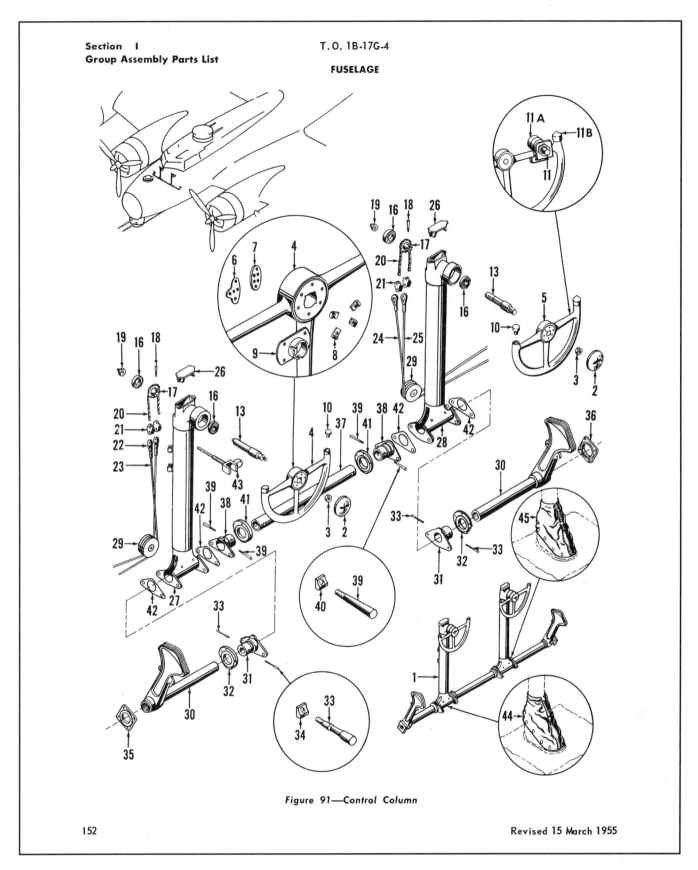

Figure 91—Control Column

B-17G manual art shows pilots' yokes connected to a common horizontal tube beneath cockpit floor. Plastic bracket (part number 9) screwed to control wheel hub to allow mounting of decorative Boeing logo cap (part number 2). (Carl Scholl/Aero Trader)

Bearing no serial number on the vertical fin, one of the first 112 B-17Es, photographed 26 September 1941, had remote belly turret with sighting blister and side scanning windows positioned just below and behind the national insignia. (SDAM)

When a manned Sperry lower ball turret was introduced on the 113th and subsequent B-17Es, redundant scanning windows were deleted. (SDAM)

tional PB-1W until 5 January 1946. Some operational patrols were flown from Newfoundland to Iceland and the Azores as a Cold War buffer against the possibility of Soviet bomber attacks. Other PB-1W missions included hurricane patrols and thunderstorm research. Turrets were generally removed from the PB-1Ws, ultimately deleting the armament that had been a reason to use Flying Fortresses in the first place. By remaining in service after most other Fortresses had been scrapped, a number of PB-1Ws survived to pass into civilian ownership as fire bombers.[8]

In 1946 the U.S. Coast Guard also received 15 or 16 B-17Gs, designated PB-1G in USCG service. A few other Coast Guard additions and deletions occurred in the postwar years of their service, the last example retiring in October 1959. Some carried lifeboats, others performed duties including photo mapping.[9]

The first [Lockheed] Vega-built B-17 was F-model serial number 42-5705, rolled out into the Burbank sun as workers looked on. Ultimately, Vega, Boeing, and Douglas all built B-17F- and G-models. (Lockheed Martin Skunk Works photo courtesy Denny Lombard)

Early Vega B-17G (42-39871) fuselage rode a traversing crane at the Lockheed Vega plant. Vertical fin assemblies had been pre-painted olive drab with yellow serials; fuselage had short-lived 1943 red-surrounded insignia, and still needed olive drab applied. Sometimes, the paint used on the pre-painted vertical fins had slightly different characteristics than the rest of the olive drab

paint, resulting in visible demarcation on finished B-17s. The G-models in this photo were still fitted with open waist windows, and, optimistically, no cheek guns since the chin turret was presumed to make them unnecessary. (SDAM)

Vega-built B-17G (42-97991), with cheek windows added, cruised over southern California. Anti-glare panel extended just beyond astrodome, instead of short panel on pre-war silver B-17s. (SDAM)

[1] "Airline Pioneer — The Boeing Model 40," by Peter M. Bowers, Pacific Northwest Aviation Historical Foundation *Journal*, Vol. 8, Pp. 2-11. [2] Peter M. Bowers, *Boeing Aircraft Since 1916*, Naval Institute Press, Annapolis, MD, 1989. [3] *Ibid.* [4] Richard G. Davis, *Carl A. Spaatz and the Air War in Europe*, Center for Air Force History, Washington, DC, 1993. [5] Peter M. Bowers, *Boeing Aircraft Since 1916*, Naval Institute Press, Annapolis, MD, 1989. [6] *Ibid.* [7] Frederick A. Johnsen, "Navy Fortresses Pioneer Early Warning Radar," *Winged Majesty — The Boeing B-17 Flying Fortress in War and Peace*, Bomber Books, Tacoma, Wash., 1980. [8] *Ibid.* [9] Scott A. Thompson, *Final Cut — The Post-war B-17 Flying Fortress: The Survivors*, Pictorial Histories, Missoula, Mont., 1990.

FIRST TO FIGHT

As European nations fought in early 1941, the still-noncombatant United States offered to make 20 B-17Cs available to the British Royal Air Force. Ostensibly intended mainly for training, these became the first Fortresses to fight when they bombed the German navy base at Wilhelmshaven on 8 July 1941.

From January through April 1941, McChord Field, near Tacoma, Washington, and south of the Boeing factory near Seattle, hosted the British Fortresses and their crews who received training from American pilots. The B-17Cs passed to the British were repainted with roundels and British serial numbers, and designated Fortress Is. RAF fin flashes were added to the vertical fins, and the rudders were painted olive drab, possibly to cover the former U.S. red-white-and-blue rudder striping. Later photos of these Fortress Is show they ultimately received camouflage paint. About 40 British aviators trained at McChord Field during this time.[1]

Charles Langmack was one of the Air Corps pilots who introduced the British to the Flying Fortress at McChord Field in 1941. As a B-18 pilot in McChord's 17th Bomb Group, Langmack, who retired from the Air Force as a colonel, had multi-engine experience, albeit half as many engines as the Fortress carried. Langmack told an interviewer: "We had one four-engine pilot on the base, a Major Pennington, I believe, and for some reason he tapped me to check out on the B-17. After I showed him that I could fly the thing, and it really wasn't a hard plane to fly, he said that we were going to train British pilots who were coming to collect a squadron of B-17Cs." Colonel Langmack recalled that Boeing was contracted to train British armorers and maintenance personnel, "while myself and another second lieutenant took care of the flight instruction at McChord. My recollection was that there were 14 flight crews involved, and right from the start it was clear that the British had sent us some very experienced pilots."[2]

Colonel Langmack said the British crews were composed of former Sunderland four-engine flying boat crews, which gave them experience with big four-engine aircraft. Langmack and the other American instructors were familiarizing the British fliers with the different instrument layout and other specifics of Fortress operation. Transitioning from water landings in Sunderlands to pavement landings in Fortresses held some surprises for the British fliers, as the big land-based American bombers often bounded back into the air following the first contact with the runway, unlike a well-planted Sunderland on the water. Colonel Langmack said his British "students" were excellent fliers in bad weather, having already experienced their share in Europe before coming to rainy western Washington state. Cross-country missions often started out in the evening from McChord, with a stop at Portland, Oregon, to the south, to shoot landings. "Portland was a pretty short field for '17s at the time, and we had the small 'toothpick' propellers that were terribly noisy," Colonel Langmack said. "I remember that the people in Portland had never heard these big four-engined things rumbling in and out, and there were lots of questions about what was going on out there." From Portland, the next stop might be Sacramento, California. On one such sortie, while climbing out from the Sacramento airfield and staying clear of a radio tower with nonfunctioning warning lights, Colonel Langmack and his British crew felt the Fortress shudder from an impact that he said "felt like we were going to knock the airplane to pieces. The noise was unbelievable." When the flight engineer returned to the cockpit from surveying the damage, he carried by the neck a large Canada goose that had ripped open the nose of the bomber. "We went back and shut down for the night. They flew a new nose down to us the next day," Colonel Langmack recalled.[3]

On other trips from Sacramento, the night mission would fly over to Spokane in eastern Washington, shooting more landings at Felts Field on the east side of town. Then it was back along the airways via Pendleton, Oregon, and back to McChord by dawn. Colonel Langmack recalled the British airmen as happy-go-lucky, and willing to laugh at their own initial awkwardness with landing the bounding

Fortresses. "They were all pretty senior fliers; they knew there weren't going to be any washouts once they got used to landing on runways," he said.[4]

ONE DOWN IN NORWAY

In September 1941, scant months after training in the United States, one of the British Fortresses lost a running battle with a German fighter over southern Norway. Nine-year-old Olav Osterhus had gone out with friends to help a farmer round up cows grazing in the woods that September morning when he spied a large airplane high in the clear sky. He assumed it was British, and only later learned it was one of the Fortress Is. Sent to search for a German pocket battleship, the Fortress was beset by a Messerschmitt Me-109 approaching in a circular movement, firing from a 45-degree angle off the rear of the bomber, Olav saw. Even from high altitude, the sound of machine guns from the dueling aircraft reached Olav's ears as he stood, mesmerized by the drama unfolding over his occupied homeland. Smoke began trailing from the Fortress, and the crew jettisoned its bomb load at about the same time as the big Boeing cranked into a steep left bank. Olav said the ground shook as the bombs detonated on a mountainside. Now in a steep dive, the smoking Fortress shed at least one piece large enough to be seen by Olav. The bomber impacted the ground; the crew perished.[5]

During the German occupa-

When Fortress Is (B-17Cs) for the British arrived at McChord Field, Washington, for training in 1941, they overflowed onto a glacial gravel parking area beyond the paved ramp. British markings included, initially, erroneously-applied serial numbers using the letters AM instead of AN on the aft fuselage just ahead of the horizontal stabilizer. (Peter M. Bowers collection)

tion, Norwegian children were told to stay away from the German soldiers; although curious about the crash site, Olav said "we didn't come near it." He said the Germans conducted a funeral service for the fallen British fliers in the village cemetery at Bygland. Olav said Norwegians were barred from the ceremony, and had to view the affair from outside the cemetery gates as the Germans and a minister laid the British to rest. Only after the war could the Norwegians build a mon-

ument to the fallen crew. After the war, Olav Osterhus finally got an opportunity to visit the Fortress crash site.[6] He had been told the Germans had removed some items for evaluation in Germany; other wreckage remained. In a twist of fate, years later Olav Osterhus moved to the United States and became mortuary services officer for McChord Air Force Base — the same base where the British Fortress Is had come from so many years earlier.

Photographed at McChord Field in natural metal finish, the British Fortress I variants later were overpainted in camouflage tones and sent into combat as the first Fortresses to fight. Sunderland flying boat crews sent to America to train in the Fortresses at McChord liked their peaceful respite in the Pacific Northwest, and proved themselves up to the task of flying in the often-challenging weather there. (Peter M. Bowers collection)

[1] "First B-17s in combat— Britons held the Fort at McChord in 1941," *The Rip Chord*, McChord Air Museum Foundation, July 1985. [2] Jay Broze, "Air Corps trained the RAF at McChord," *The Rip Chord*, McChord Air Museum Foundation, July 1985. [3] *Ibid.* [4] *Ibid.* [5] Frederick A. Johnsen, "McChord Employee watched RAF Fortress crash in Norway," *The Rip Chord*, McChord Air Museum Foundation, July 1985. [6] *Ibid.*

In Harm's Way

Prevailing thought in the U.S. Army Air Corps, as well as in the Royal Air Force, in the 1930s embraced daylight precision bombardment as the means to end wars by crippling an enemy's ability and will to fight. The architects of precision bombardment in the Air Corps succeeded in bringing their ideas to the forefront; the impressive performance of pre-war B-17s fueled their beliefs that unescorted heavy bombers were capable of waging war without fighter cover. The same confidence that sustained the B-17 through initial procurement hurdles found the Air Corps wanting for escort fighters a few short years later when Messerschmitt Me-109s and Mitsubishi A6M Zeros demonstrated how far fighter development had come since the Fortress first took wing in 1935. The problem was daunting: Most major air powers, including the United States, had placed faith in short-range interceptors to counter enemy air action. When such interceptors proved capable of extracting a serious toll on unescorted bomber formations, a latter-day effort to stretch the range of the Army Air Forces' premier pursuit planes prompted the use of underwing pylons for drop tanks to allow American fighters to carry more gasoline.

The zenith of this development was realized when an additional internal fuselage tank was added to the P-51B Mustang; coupled with two underwing tanks, the Mustang could be with the heavy bombers deep in Germany for the first time in 1944, following initial escorting inroads in December 1943. In a fundamental way, the successes and accolades given to the B-17 for its role in the skies over Europe are linked directly to the evolution and success of the P-51 as an escort fighter.

BY THE NUMBERS

The U.S. Army Air Forces authored a statistical digest shortly after the end of World War Two, capturing informative data about aircraft and aircrew production and deployment. The tallies give testimony to the spread of Fortresses in different combat areas during the war. The number of B-17 crews on hand in the European Theater of Operations (ETO) as of the end of June 1943 was 408, compared with only 47 B-24 crews in the ETO at the same time. By the end of the year, 1,472 B-17 crews were in the ETO, as were 609 B-24 crews. The maximum number of Fortress crews in the ETO was achieved in March 1945, when 2,850 B-17 crews were tallied there; highest number of B-24 crews in the ETO was 1,734, achieved by the end of June 1944 (when the total number of B-17 crews in that theater was only slightly higher, at 1,816). In the Mediterranean Theater of Operations (MTO), the number of B-17 crews on hand as of the end of June 1943 was 169, compared with 74 B-24 crews in that theater. Maximum number of B-17 crews in the MTO was 669, attained by the end of January 1945. High point in the number of B-24 crews assigned to the MTO was 1,753, more than 1,000 more than the highest number of Fortress crews in the theater. The AAF statistics for crews on hand in various theaters only began with the last half of 1943. By that time, the statisticians logged no B-17 crews in Pacific

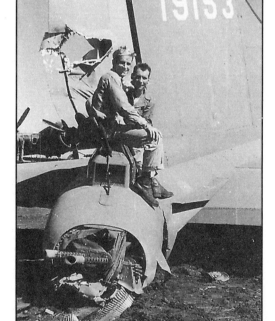

Tokyo Taxi, B-17E 41-9153 of the Fifth Bomb Group, sustained battle damage that resulted in tailwheel failure on landing, causing the tailgun compartment to wrench loose and spew .50-caliber ammunition in the turf behind the careening Fortress. (Joe Voellmeck)

Ocean areas, Far East Air Forces, China-Burma-India (CBI), and Alaska for the remainder of the war. (This tabulation evidently excluded specialized VIP and search-and-rescue Fortresses, on hand in small numbers.) In a category loosely identified as "other overseas theaters", the statistical digest logged 36 B-17 crews as of the end of June 1943, and none listed most of the other months of the war, except for February and March 1944, when seven B-17 crews were tallied here. (This may reflect the absence of available data, or it may denote the withdrawal of B-17s from areas other than the European and Mediterranean theaters.)[1]

Tallies of B-17s in the continental

FLYING SAFETY

Air Force statistics for aircraft accidents in the continental United States, from 1942 through August 1945, include the following extracted numbers:[6]

	B-17	B-24	B-25	P-39	P-40	P-47
1942						
All accidents	146	123	151	414	798	106
Airplanes wrecked	46	46	66	171	202	41
Rate/100,000 hrs.	55	75	104	351	507	245
1943						
All accidents	539	457	284	904	1,070	958
Airplanes wrecked	182	240	139	403	285	380
Rate/100,000 hrs.	39	39	44	228	297	163
1944						
All accidents	638	779	239	590	1,280	1,303
Airplanes wrecked	203	359	123	278	360	474
Rate/100,000 hrs.	25	33	24	228	127	122
1945 (Jan.-Aug.)						
All accidents	266	354	247	26	421	682
Airplanes wrecked	48	101	118	13	120	230
Rate/100,000 hrs.	23	29	24	156	115	97

Relative rates of mishaps suffered in B-17s and B-24s may reflect degrees of difficulty crews faced in mastering these two heavy bomber types.

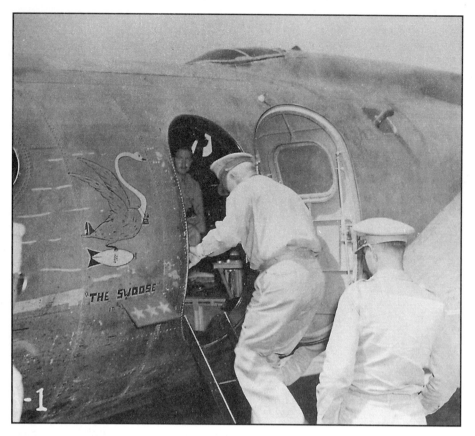

General Brett boarded the celebrated B-17D The Swoose *in the Pacific. Round door was squared and moved aft beginning with B-17E. (SDAM)*

Total Flying Fortresses on hand in the Air Force in November 1941 was 145; next month this was up to 198 Fortresses. B-17s in the USAAF inventory peaked at 4,574 in August 1944, and tapered off, diminishing nearly every month up to August 1945, when the AAF B-17 inventory was placed at 3,677 of the bombers.[3]

Boeing production of B-17s at the company's plant beside Boeing Field in Seattle totaled 6,942 Flying Fortresses accepted between 1940 and August 1945. For 1940, this represented only 53 Fortresses. By 1941 this grew to 144 factory acceptances of B-17s; in 1942, 1,259 B-17s were accepted at the Seattle factory; in 1943 the figure swelled to 2,340 B-17s from Seattle; by 1944 the high mark of 2,837 Seattle B-17s was recorded. In 1945, with the company's production emphasis shifted to B-29s, factory acceptances of B-17s at Boeing was down to 309 Fortresses. When Douglas Aircraft began building B-17s under contract at

United States are revealing: As of November 1941, 84 Fortresses were in the Air Force in the United States. This figure broke one thousand in February 1943, when 1,082 Forts were tallied stateside. The stateside peak inventory reached 2,386 B-17s in July 1944 as production thrived; the numbers diminished, likely due to a combination of sending more Fortresses to Europe and retiring early stateside trainers. By April 1945, the inventory of USAAF B-17s in the continental United States had dipped to 880 aircraft. The end of the war in Europe saw B-17s released from that part of the world. Likely due to returnees as well as bottled-up new production B-17s after VE-Day, the stateside inventory climbed to 1,907 by June, and 2,405 by August 1945. By

December 1945, this had dropped to 665 B-17s in stateside Air Force inventory, evidence of the dismantling of the air armada of World War Two.[2]

B-17E Calamity Jane was photographed at the 13th Air Depot Group area on New Caledonia on 5 November 1943. Pacific B-17 operations were in decline by that time, and socketless gun ports suggest this Fortress was out of combat by the time this photograph was taken. (USAF)

Long Beach, California, in 1942, factory acceptances were 85 that first year. By 1943, factory acceptances of Douglas-built B-17s was 952; in 1944 the Douglas figure peaked at 1,271 factory acceptances of B-17s; for 1945, through August, the tally was 692 Douglas Fortresses. Lockheed (Vega), the third participant in the BVD (Boeing-Vega-Douglas) B-17 production pool, logged 68 B-17 factory acceptances in 1942, 887 in 1943, 1,244 in 1944, and 551 up through August 1945.[4]

The AAF determined the average cost for B-17s procured between 1939 and 1945. From 1939-41, a Flying Fortress cost $301,221. As quantities increased in 1942, the unit price dropped to $258,949. AAF statistics were not posted for 1943, but in 1944 a B-17 cost an average of $204,370. Bargain B-17s were those turned out in 1945 at an average of $187,742.[5]

BEST AIRPLANE FOR THE JOB

The majority of three thousand officers and enlisted men in Eighth Air Force heavy bomber crews tallied between 28 May and 5 June 1944 said their aircraft — be they B-17s or B-24s — were the best for the job. When separated into B-17 and B-24 crews, 92 percent of the surveyed B-17 crews said they had the best type of machine, compared with 76 percent of the polled B-24 crews who said they had the best type of aircraft. As the survey summary noted: "The proportion who are 'sold' on their own plane is... greater among B-17 crew members."[7]

The survey presented other conclusions about Eighth Air Force crews and their two types of heavy bombers: "In both B-17 and B-24 crews, men who are convinced their type of ship is best are more likely than other men to express satisfaction with their jobs. In B-24 crews, the bombardiers, navigators, and co-pilots appear somewhat less likely than other crew members to feel they have the best type of airplane. In B-17 crews, men in the different crew positions do not differ appreciably in the appraisal they give their ship." The study emphasized that "B-17 and B-24 crews do not differ in their belief in the importance of the job they are doing," and that the two types of crews did not differ "in their expressed willingness to take on another series of missions nor in the proportions who say they would sign up for combat flying if they were starting all over again."[8]

Interestingly, in both B-17s and B-24s, co-pilots were the least likely to answer "yes" to the question, "Do you think you have the best type of airplane for the particular job which you have to do?" The 1944 survey drew no inference from this statistic, although a latter-day assessment might conclude that of all crew positions, only co-pilots have a built-in job dissatisfaction linked with their ambitions to become pilots. In the survey, the total sample of 3,000 crewmen might yield only 100 to 200 in any one crew position for each type of bomber, and the surveyors cautioned that this small sample "must be regarded as suggestive, rather than conclusive evidence of a real difference between crew positions existing in the total Eighth Air Force heavy bomber crews from which this cross-section sample was drawn." By crew position, those who said "yes" that theirs was the best type of airplane for the partic-

Fifth Bomb Group B-17 co-pilot Joe Voellmeck pointed his camera across the nacelles of his Fortress as a Zero rolled in for a gunnery attack during a bombing mission to Bougainville's Shortland Harbor late in 1942. (Joe Voellmeck)

Dramatically illuminated view of the nose of a B-17E shows metal knockout door for cleaning bombsight glass. Sockets in nose fit .30-caliber machine gun; larger .50-caliber guns required bracing. Tube extending down from underside of nose at left is drift sight. (Peter M. Bowers collection)

Engineers for both types of bombers posted high satisfaction rates. Again, while the 1944 survey did not endeavor to explain this phenomenon, an after-the-fact observation might conclude that engineers on both types of heavy bomber received intense technical training on their particular aircraft, and were intimately familiar with its systems and functions, possibly generating a high degree of confidence as a result of this knowledge and training.

The markedly higher satisfaction rates expressed by B-17 navigators and bombardiers than their B-24 counterparts may be attributed to the generally roomier nose section in a B-17. For these crew members, working conditions were better in a Flying Fortress. An extreme example of this was the grafting of a complete B-17G nose to a B-24J in the U.S. for evaluation. While the hybrid bomber had poor flying characteristics, an AAF evaluation commented favorably, and probably wryly, on the improved working area for the navigator and bombardier in this particular B-24!

Interestingly, absent from the 1944 survey report was any suggestion that the surveyed crewmen thought either the B-17 or the B-24 was more combat-survivable than the other type of bomber, although one B-24 crewman commented on cramped quarters in the nose impeding fast bailouts.

Statistics compiled by the AAF in 1944 showed a rising trend in the average number of sorties per month per crew assigned to operational groups in the Eighth Air Force. In November 1943 (the first month of the survey), the average number of sorties for the month for

ular job they had to do produced the following numbers for the survey:

(PERCENTAGE WHO SAY YES)

CO-PILOTS
B-24 Crews	58%
B-17 Crews	88%

NAVIGATORS
B-24 Crews	63%
B-17 Crews	93%

BOMBARDIERS
B-24 Crews	65%
B-17 Crews	93%

ENGINEERS
B-24 Crews	91%
B-17 Crews	93%

PILOTS, RADIO OPERATORS, AND GUNNERS
B-24 Crews	79%
B-17 Crews	92%

MEN IN ALL CREW POSITIONS COMBINED
B-24 Crews	76%
B-17 Crews	92%

Pilots, radio operators, and gunners were tallied together because, the survey said, they showed "no appreciable difference" in their responses to the question.[9]

WARBIRD**TECH** SERIES

B-24 crews was about two; for B-17 crews the average was about 2.8. B-17 crew sortie rates remained higher than B-24 rates until April 1944, when Eighth AF B-24 crews posted an average of seven sorties per month per crew, compared with the B-17 crews' average somewhere near 6.6 sorties a month. By May 1944, the last month of the chart, B-24 crew sorties averaged around 8.3, while B-17 crew sorties averaged about 7.4, within the limitations of the graph. Clearly, the number of sorties was increasing for both types of bomber crew.[10]

The debate over merits of B-17s versus B-24s began when the two airplanes were new, and

Fifth Air Force B-17E RFD Tojo (41-2627) received outdoor engine maintenance on 10 May 1943, prior to flying a reconnaissance sortie over Rabaul. Unique B-17 engine nacelle camouflage demarcation lip is evident, with gray receding back from the ring of the cowling. (Bushnell collection)

B-17E Sally *stripped back to bare metal sported extra windows in the fuselage. This Fortress, number 41-2633, was the aircraft used for transportation by Fifth Air Force commander Gen. George C. Kenney.* (Larry Jaynes collection)

will linger long after publication of this volume. There is evidence to suggest the USAAF even fueled the controversy while trying to instill pride in each type of bomber crew. Some editions of the pilot's manual for the B-17, when explaining go-around procedures for landings, accompany the text with a drawing of a crashed B-24 on the runway blocking the B-17's intended landing. Similarly, the same section in some B-24 pilot manuals shows a crashed B-17 as the cause of the B-24's go-around!

Eighth Air Force B-17F Lightning Strikes *had the nose Plexiglas modified to take a braced .50-caliber machine gun. Slightly darker hue in upper part of nose is recess to accommodate gun mount.* (USAF)

In one of war's greatest ironies, Air Force B-17s were exposed to combat at the outset, when unarmed B-17Ds from California arrived over Hawaii in the midst of the Japanese attack 7 December 1941. American Fortresses immediately went into battle in the days following Pearl Harbor in the Pacific. The following samples of Fortress combat in World War Two, while not exhaustive, serve to illuminate the B-17's war:

On 8 December 1941, B-17s at Clark Field in the Philippines were sent aloft in anticipation of a Japanese air raid, to keep them from being ground targets. When the Forts had to land for more fuel, they were caught on the ground in an air raid. After Japanese air attacks the following day, Far East Air Forces (FEAF) B-17 strength was diminished from 35 to 17 Fortresses in commission.

Capt. Colin Kelly piloted one of the B-17s that sortied on 10 December to attack a Japanese convoy that was putting troops and equipment ashore at Vigan and at Aparri on Luzon. Captain Kelly pressed an attack on a warship first identified as a battleship, and later proven to be the heavy cruiser Ashigara. On returning to Clark Field, Kelly's Fortress was set upon by Japanese fighters that shot the bomber down. Posthumously, Colin Kelly was awarded the Distinguished Service Cross (DSC) for sinking a battleship, although his actual attack probably yielded near-misses on the cruiser.[11] There's no doubt that Colin Kelly and the others performed bravely in the opening

When the right main gear collapsed, the solid aluminum Hamilton-Standard propeller blades on engines three and four bent back as this training B-17G settled to a stop at Las Vegas Army Airfield, Nevada. (Marty Isham)

days of World War Two in the Pacific. The need for heroes was great in that desperate hour, and whatever subsequent study of the battle revealed, it sustained the picture of young Fortress crews discharging their duties stoically in the face of onrushing Japanese air and naval forces.

By 11 December, B-17s at Hawaii were contributing to regular search missions aiming to sound the alarm in the face of any returning Japanese forces; only submarines were ever found. On 14 December, B-17s attacked the Japanese beachhead at Legaspi. Returning with a shot-up Fortress, 1 Lt. Hewitt Wheless made a crash landing at Cagayan that ultimately earned him a DSC. On 17 December, Fortresses from

the Philippines were evacuating Luzon for Batchelor Field, Australia. From Batchelor, nine B-17s staged a shuttle mission on 22 December 1941, attacking ships in Davao Bay before landing at Del Monte in the Philippines. On 24 December, three Forts departed Del Monte to bomb airfield and shipping targets at Davao, recovering at Batchelor.[12]

A handwritten notation found in one of the aircraft evacuating the Philippines listed serial numbers of 19th Bomb Group B-17s arriving at

Malang, Java, for duty on 30 December 1941 as: B-17C 40-2062; B-17Ds 40-3061, 3097, 3067, 3070, 3078, 3079, 3066, 3074, and 3064. The notation also listed 19th Bomb Group B-17s on hand in January-February 1942 as including: B-17Es 41-2472, 2460, 2469, 2478, 2458, 2470, 2453, 2488, and 2498. Another unidentified B-17E and an unidentified B-17D were also tallied in the log, which ultimately was placed in the Air Force Historical Research Agency archives.[13]

Tinker Toy, a B-17F of the 381st Bomb Group based near Ridgewell, England, was photographed in August 1943 with substantial nose damage; maintenance man points to a hit on the windscreen corner post as well. Though an F-model, Tinker Toy has its cheek guns staggered in the pattern later used by B-17Gs, with the left gun forward. Style of window also

attempts to gain more forward coverage for the cheek gun than earliest flush cheek mounts. (USAF)

Placed on the Poorman gunnery range at Las Vegas Army Airfield, Nevada, this B-17 Sperry top turret conserved ammunition costs by using .30-caliber machine guns for training. (Marty Isham)

Sweeney continued to operate from Canton and Nandi in support of Task Group 8.9 until returning to Hawaii on 30 January. Significant was the knowledge gained about long overwater navigation legs and servicing aircraft in far-flung operations — operations the USAAF would find necessary to the prosecution of the Pacific war over the next four years.

On 1 February 1942, VIII Bomber Command was activated at Langley Field, Virginia. This would result in creation of the archetypal B-17 bombardment organizations, those heavy bomb groups of the Eighth Air Force which were to be equipped with Fortresses. But for the time, USAAF B-17 combat was a Pacific venture. On 9 February, a dozen B-17s from Seventh Air Force were detached and made available for assignment to Task Force 11 in the South Pacific. On the 14th of the month, a solo Seventh AF B-17 flew a photo reconnaissance mission to Wake Island. On 23 February 1942, Fifth Air Force B-17s from Townsville flew their first mission against the Japanese base at Rabaul; inclement weather and mechanical problems dwindled the strike force to only one B-17 dropping bombs over the target. Four days later, all available Fifth Air Force B-17s joined LB-30 export Liberators and other warplanes in the Battle of Java Sea, but the Japanese convoy moving in from the northeast was not turned back by either air or naval power. In the face of Japanese movement, the last Fifth Air Force heavy bomber mission flown out of Java was launched on 1 March. (Some Air Force records list operations only as "heavy bomber," inadvertently obscuring whether the action involved B-17s,

Targets at Davao Bay and Japanese forces landing at the island of Tarakan received attention from B-17s in the first two weeks of January 1942. On 16 January, Lt. Col. Walter C. Sweeney began the first significant dispatch of aircraft from Hawaiian assets when he led six B-17s to Palmyra. The following day the Forts moved on to Canton Island, where they executed submarine patrols for the next two days. Meanwhile, FEAF B-17s operating from Malang targeted shipping and an airfield. Between 22 January and 3 February, the FEAF B-17s at Malang performed about 15 missions against Japanese shipping in Makassar Strait. Six of the missions produced negative results, four aborted for bad weather, and on five of the missions, despite heavy losses, the B-17s claimed four ships sunk.[14]

The Fortresses led by Colonel

Liberators, or a combination of the two types.) The following day, five B-17s and three LB-30s participated in the evacuation of the last men at Jogjakarta, the final airfield on Java not already in the hands of the Japanese, who were only 20 miles away.

The urgent need to establish air forces across the Pacific saw General Brereton arrive in India on 5 March to take command of 10th Air Force, whose combat force listed only eight B-17s at the time. Much as pre-war Air Corps exercises had used B-18 bombers to transport military equipment, on 8 March the few Fortresses of 10th Air Force were employed in a transport role, moving 29 tons of supplies and 474 troops from India to Magwe, and, on the return flights, carrying 423 civilian evacuees.

A 20 March 1942 report by General Ira Eaker outlined basic ways in which proposed American daylight precision bombing of Europe was compatible and complementary with British night area bombing; a cooperative Allied bomber offensive was in the offing. Meanwhile, around the world, on 26 March, three 19th Bomb Group B-17s were the long-range couriers that evacuated Philippine President Quezon and his family to Australia to keep them from Japanese capture. On 3 April, six heavy bombers from the fledgling 10th Air Force bombed docks and warehouses at Rangoon; three large fires were observed as a result, and one B-17 was missing. On 12 April, single-ship B-17 strikes launched from Mindanao targeted Nichols Field and the harbor at Cebu. In a turnabout on the stereotype of American daylight bombing, on 15 April six Fortresses from 10th Air Force

Wolverine, *an early Eighth Air Force B-17G with no cheek guns and older F-style Plexiglas nose, had four bombing missions credited when a belly landing bent the props and pushed the lightweight aluminum chin turret tub back.* (Bob Sturges collection)

launched a night raid from Dum Dum Airfield near Calcutta, using flares to guide them over a Rangoon target. The flash of searchlights over the target area made bomb damage assessment impossible for the B-17 crews. Another night raid by four 10th Air Force B-17s on 5 May targeted parked airplanes and a hangar at Mingaladon; while crews made damage claims, accurate assessment was

again not possible. Next night, three 10th AF Fortresses returned to Mingaladon Airfield, scoring hits on a fuel dump. Also on 6 May, B-17s from Fifth Air Force tried without success to sink Japanese shipping in the vicinity of Bougainville.[15]

On 12 May 1942, B-17s were employed in an effort to block Japanese aircraft from interrupting

Belly landing a B-17 with the ball turret in place could do serious damage. Crews took to jettisoning the ball turret when time allowed before making a belly landing. This wrinkled Fortress is B-17G 42-31105 (a Boeing product) of the Eighth AF, photographed on 30 December 1943. (Bob Sturges collection)

Employing a name sometimes derisively used to portray light postwar general aviation aircraft, Spamcan of the 381st Bomb Group shows evidence of having cheek guns installed after the aircraft was built; hence the darker, newer olive drab paint on the cheek framing. (USAF)

the Allied air cargo route to China. Tenth Air Force dispatched four B-17s from Dum Dum Airfield to bomb Japanese aircraft and facilities at newly-captured Myitkyina. Several parked airplanes were torched, and runways were damaged. Myitkyina and its Japanese aerial force posed a threat to the Allied field at Dinjan. During the month, Fifth Air Force B-17s repeatedly bombed targets at Rabaul and Lae.

On the 18th of May, Seventh Air Force went on alert because of the potential for a Japanese attack on Midway. Augmenting B-17s on search missions were barrel-shaped twin-engine Douglas B-18s; during this period, the 72nd Bomb Squadron of the Fifth Bomb Group turned its B-18s in for B-17s. A Flying Fortress from 11th Air Force flew the first armed reconnaissance mission to launch from the airfield

built in secret at Umnak, but found no sign of the Japanese in the Aleutians. Japanese offensive efforts at this time were coordinated between the Aleutians and Midway in an effort to split American forces and confuse planners. On 30 May, Seventh Air Force began flying B-17s from Hawaii to Midway in anticipation of a naval-borne attack there. The next day, the 7th Air Force Flying Fortresses on detached service at Midway began search missions. On 2 June, a half-dozen of 16 Fortresses on detached service at Midway were rotated back to Hawaii. Next day, first action in the battle of Midway saw nine B-17s from that island attack five major ships 570 miles distant; several hits and near misses were claimed. Seven additional B-17s left Oahu to supplant those already at Midway. On the morning of 4 June, 14 Seventh Air Force Flying Fortresses engaged a Japanese task

force 145 miles from Midway and closing. That afternoon, two B-17s attacked an aircraft carrier force; four other Fortresses claimed a hit on a heavy cruiser 185 miles from Midway. Six B-17s, arriving from Hawaii, bombed ships about 170 miles from Midway. On 5 June, the battle of Midway continued, with American airpower chasing a retiring Japanese fleet. That day, eight B-17s bombed a force of ships about 130 miles from the island, claiming hits on two large warships. In the afternoon, six Fortresses were said to hit a cruiser 300 miles from Midway. The final strike of the Midway action by Seventh Air Force aircraft was a five-Fortress attack on a heavy cruiser 425 miles distant. One B-17 succumbed to Japanese gunfire and another ran out of gas. The island of Midway never fell, although installations there were damaged by Japanese bombs. During the action, Seventh Air Force mounted 16 Flying Fortress attacks, totaling 55 sorties with the B-17s.[16]

Midway produced mixed reviews for the B-17 operations. Later analysis indicated the Fortresses did not sink the major warships they attacked. Touted in pre-war years as coastal protectors, B-17s (and B-24s) often returned from strikes against Japanese fleets with disappointing results as the vessels wheeled and turned to avoid the falling bombs. And yet, the contribution of B-17s to the American victory at Midway cannot be discounted. Rightly portrayed as the finest hour for Navy SBD Dauntless dive bombers that sank four Japanese aircraft carriers, Midway owes some of its outcome to the B-17s just the same. Combined Fifth and 11th Bomb Group B-17Es arrived at Midway first, followed by replenish-

ing Fortresses from the 42nd Bombardment Squadron that included a pair of older small-tailed B-17Ds, according to retired Maj. Gen. Brooke E. Allen, who led the 42nd Squadron to Midway. "I had a couple of Ds," General Allen recalled during an interview in the 1970s. "We just tucked them in out of the way."[17]

By 12:30 p.m. on 3 June, several sightings of Japanese ship movements prompted the first launch of B-17s to counter them. By 4:30 that afternoon, Col. Walter C. Sweeney's Fortress formation wheeled in behind the Japanese fleet to make an attack from out of the sun. Sweeney took his three-plane element of the Fortress formation in to attack at only 8,000 feet. When the Fortress runs were finished, scant damage had been done, and the main body of aircraft carriers had not been located by the B-17s. After straggling in as late as 9:45 that night, Fortress crews at Midway readied themselves for more sorties the following day. On 4 June, with B-17s already en route to the fleet that did not include aircraft carriers, word was received that the carriers had been located. Colonel Sweeney's Fortresses then changed heading to close with the important aircraft carriers. As the big Fortresses were droning toward the Japanese carriers, the warplanes already launched by the carriers struck Midway Island furiously. With the Japanese aircraft carriers heavily defended in a large armada, Colonel Sweeney's Fortresses made their attacks from 20,000 feet this time. Even as the Fortress crews scanned the huge fleet for the locations of the aircraft carriers, the Japanese fleet began evasive turns to shake off low-level attacks by Vought Vindi-

When *Five Grand* of the 96th Bomb Group belly landed at Honington, England in 1944, the ADF football-shaped antenna housing ripped free and tore holes in the famous Fortress' signature-laden hide. (Bob Sturges collection)

cators. Capt. Cecil Faulkner of the Fifth Bomb Group was the first to spot the carriers, and he led his three-plane element in for a bomb run. The search for the carriers among the fleet had spread out the B-17 formation to the point where attacks were made by three-ship elements and sometimes single B-17s, instead of a massed formation. The smaller bomb pattern afforded by a three-ship formation made it easier for the Japanese carriers to maneuver and avoid the falling bombs. Even at 20,000 feet, flak holed the Fortresses. Zeros

In September 1943, two B-17Es (nearest camera) flew formation with an F-model during training out of Lockbourne Army Air Base, Ohio. Two styles of national insignia are in evidence. (USAF)

Eighth Air Force B-17Fs dropped sticks of bombs over a German target in a photo that captured the essence of American daylight bombardment. Visible open bomb bay doors sometimes tipped off German fighter pilots about the timing of their quarry's bomb run. (USAF via SDAM)

made some passes at the B-17s. The serendipity for the Americans was the timing of the arrival of the B-17s, and the subsequent discovery of the location of the aircraft carriers in the enemy fleet just as the Japanese carrier aircraft were trying to land on the ships after the morning raid on Midway. Analysis of the battle suggests none of the more than 320 bombs dropped by B-17s during Midway fighting hit a Japanese ship, although near-misses inflicted some damage. "Admittedly, we weren't very accurate, but we kept the carriers going in circles," General Allen said. As the air-

craft carriers maneuvered to avoid the B-17s' bombs, frantic Japanese fighter pilots, their airplanes low on gas, tried to land on the decks of the carriers while they were turning. American aircraft flying at altitudes lower than the Fortresses watched as Japanese aircraft smashed into the turning carriers, or ditched into the sea. "We just sprayed bombs down there, hoping to get hits." By doing this, the Fortress crews caused the Japanese carriers to make the hard evasive turns that denied some of the Japanese pilots a chance to land as long as the Fortresses were in the

vicinity. "That was our main contribution," explained General Allen.[18]

As the Midway battle was reeling toward an American victory on 5 June, 10 B-17s of 11th Air Force participated in search and attack sorties in Alaska. Using radar, the Fortresses bombed what they thought to be ships, but what actually were portions of the Pribilof Islands. The days following Midway were busy for 11th Air Force, with mixed gaggles including B-17s making repeat attacks on Kiska when the harsh Aleutian weather allowed. The last day of June 1942 saw a lone B-17 from 11th Air Force perform weather reconnaissance over Kiska; that day, Fifth Air Force B-17s attacked Koepang, Dili, and Kendari.[19]

On the first day of July 1942, the first B-17 of Operation Bolero, the aerial delivery of aircraft to Europe via the North Atlantic route, landed at Prestwick on its journey. Next day, B-17s in North Africa joined B-24s as United States Army Middle East Air Forces (USAMEAF) heavy bombers raided Tobruk Harbor at night. The Fortresses returned the next night to bomb supplies at Tobruk. Creating a trickle that would become a deluge, the second B-17 to arrive in the United Kingdom via the North Atlantic ferry route arrived on the 4th of July 1942. On 16 July, Fortresses of the 11th Bomb Group began the flight from Hawaii to the South Pacific. Next day, USAMEAF B-17s attacked Tobruk, Fifth AF Fortresses bombed Rabaul's harbor, and 11th Air Force sent three B-17s and seven B-24s on weather, bombing, and photo reconnaissance missions to targets including Kiska. Japanese fighters caught and downed one of the 11th AF Fortresses over the

Aleutians. By mid-1942, B-17s were carrying the war to the enemy in the Central and South Pacific, the middle east, and the Aleutians, while preparations were underway in England for the definitive massive use of Flying Fortresses.

Near the end of July 1942, the 97th Bomb Group was the first American heavy bomb group to assemble in the United Kingdom with air and ground echelons. And on the last day of the month, Fifth Air Force B-17s attacked Gona and a transport nearby, and bombed Kukum Beach and a landing strip at Lunga on the north coast of Guadalcanal, as American invasion troops left Fiji, bound for the Solomon Islands. That same day, nine B-17s of the 11th Bomb Group, led by Col. LaVerne G. Saunders, also targeted the area around the landing strip at Lunga on Guadalcanal. By 7 August, the force of available B-17s in Fifth Air Force had grown to permit a formation of 13 from the 19th Bomb Group to attack Vunakanau's airfield in coordination with the landing of Marines on Guadalcanal. Though small by later standards, this mission, like the Seventh Air Force Midway efforts that preceded it, showed a growth in American bombardment presence in the Pacific. While B-17s, including some F-models, would continue to fly combat in the Pacific into 1943, the USAAF would ultimately concentrate its B-17s in England and Italy, while replacing early Pacific Fortresses with Liberators. Between 8 and 23 August, South Pacific (SOPAC) B-17s logged search missions over the lower Solomon Islands, looking for any attempt by the Japanese to pull off a surprise attack on the forces that were then consolidating the Guadalcanal beachhead.[20]

FIRST EIGHTH AIR FORCE B-17 MISSION

The 17th day of August 1942 marked the introduction of USAAF B-17s from England over western Europe as a dozen Fortresses from the 97th Bomb Group, with Royal Air Force Spitfire escort, bombed the marshaling yards at Rouen-Sotteville. Defending his B-17 on the Rouen-Sotteville raid, Sgt. Kent R. West shot down an attacking German fighter, becoming the first Eighth Air Force gunner credited for a combat victory. Two days later, the ambitious Eighth Air Force put 22 Fortresses over the Abbeville/Drucat area, bombing

A taxiing accident at Las Vegas, Nevada, on 24 July 1944 punched this B-17G's propellers into a North American AT-6 Texan trainer canopy and wing. The mishap Fortress had cheek gun installed on right side only. (Via Marty Isham)

On 28 March 1943, sheetmetal damage to the tail turret of the B-17F *Memphis Belle was photographed. The Memphis Belle is permanently displayed in the city of Memphis, Tennessee as of this writing.*

airfield facilities and intending to draw German fighters who then would not be able to oppose a simultaneous Allied ground assault probing the continent at Dieppe. As August grew old, the Eighth Air Force made more Fortress raids over France and the Low Countries, guided by a codified cooperation agreement with the RAF.[21]

Near Guadalcanal in August, dive bombers and heavy bombers attacked a Japanese convoy carrying an invasion force there. On the 25th of the month, Fortresses from Espiritu Santo enjoyed a victory when they sank the destroyer Mutsuki. By mid-day, the Japanese force was withdrawing to the north.

On 5 September, responding to urgent statements from General Spaatz, General Eisenhower relented on a plan to suspend Eighth Air Force operations from England in order to support the impending campaign in North Africa. Eisenhower said he considered air operations from the United Kingdom and North Africa mutually complementary. (However, in 1943, Eighth Air Force would again complain as assets, particularly B-24 groups, were temporarily sent to North Africa.) Also on 5 September, Eighth Air Force launched 31 B-17s to bomb a locomotive center at the Rouen-Sotteville marshaling yards, making this the largest Eighth AF attack to date. First combat losses for the Eighth Air Force's VIII Bomber Command came on 6 September when two B-17s were downed by fighters over Meaulte, where 30 Fortresses had gone to bomb the Avions Potez aircraft plant being used by the Germans. As the Eighth Air Force and the Luftwaffe appraised each other during these early operations, B-17 crews came back from combat on 7 September claiming a dozen German planes shot down. That day, seven of 29 B-17s launched made an ineffective raid on shipyards at Rotterdam in poor weather, while two more Fortresses went after targets of opportunity around Utrecht.[22]

In the Pacific, B-17s continued to work with twin-engine bombers

Belly-landed Eighth Air Force B-17G shows chin turret controller in stowed position in the left of the nose (the right from within the airplane). Darker paint around cheek gun window suggests it was a post-production installation. (Bob Sturges collection)

Telltale fingers of contrails point out a 15th Air Force B-17G formation. Contrails aided Axis gunners in finding the Americans by day. (Don Hayes collection)

and dive bombers in attacks on Japanese ships. On 11 September 1942, a Fifth Air Force B-17 planted a bomb directly on the stern of the destroyer Yayoi, later known to have sunk. The next day, a Fifth AF Fortress engaged in strafing runs on a Japanese vessel in the Bismarck Sea; the Pacific war of the B-17 was not all high-altitude formation precision bombardment, as the war over Europe was characterized.[23]

Between 18 September and 30 November, Fifth Air Force B-17s totaled 180 sorties against Rabaul. But the era of the B-17 in the Pacific was waning; Gen. George C. Kenney, Fifth Air Force commander, was aware his Fortresses were slated to be replaced by new B-24 Liberators. In Fifth AF, the first B-24 mission was mounted by the pioneering 90th Bomb Group on 16 November 1942.[24]

On 2 October 1942, Eighth Air Force sent 30 B-17s over the Avions Potez factory at Meaulte again, as a small group attacked Saint Omer/Longuenesse airfield. Allied escort fighters numbering about 400 were breached by German

fighters, but, according to Air Force accounts, the B-17s defended themselves well. (Such would not always be the case as the Luftwaffe devised new tactics including slashing head-on passes at the bombers instead of runs from behind, where the bombers' defenses and slower relative closing speeds made the German fighters more vulnerable.) An 11 October sighting of a Japanese task force by SOPAC B-17s alerted friendly surface vessels that drove the Japanese force away, again underscoring the great utility of B-17s as long-ranging search platforms in the South Pacific. But the future of the Flying Fortress was in the skies over Europe. On 21 October, VIII Bomber Command sent B-17s and B-24s on the first mission against U-boat pens, at Lorient-Keroman.[25] All but the 97th Bomb Group's B-17s turned back in the face of inclement weather. The 15 Fortresses put up by the 97th found a hole in the cloud cover and descended through it, flying at only 17,500 feet over the sub pens, 5,000 to 10,000 feet lower than most attacks had been made by the Eighth. Thirty-six Focke-Wulf FW-

190s attacked the B-17s; three Fortresses were shot down.[26] Submarine pens would prove to be expensive targets that were hard to damage due to their heavy concrete construction. On 31 October, General Spaatz informed USAAF chief Gen. Henry "Hap" Arnold that operations against the pens could be too costly for the results achieved. General Spaatz contemplated going in as low as 4,000 feet, and risking heavier losses for the possibility of more decisive results. A critical test came on 9 November when Eighth Air Force sent a dozen B-24s over the U-boat base at St. Nazaire at altitudes ranging from 17,500 to 18,300 feet, while 31 B-17s went in at 7,500 to 10,000 feet. The B-24s suffered little anti-aircraft damage as they flew higher than the Fortresses; the B-17s lost three of their force to flak, while 22 other B-17s were damaged. No more low-level heavy bomber attacks on submarine bases were made.[27]

On 28 October 1942, USAMEAF Fortresses sought a convoy in the Mediterranean, but did not find it, bombing cruisers in Pylos Bay instead. The maritime reconnais-

Eighth AF's Tugboat Annie, an old B-17F missing its turrets when photographed, showed evidence of nose and prop damage. (Harry Fisher)

sance career of the Flying Fortress was again highlighted on 12 November when a SOPAC B-17 sighted a Japanese aircraft carrier 350 miles from Guadalcanal and maintained contact with the enemy vessel for two hours, during which the B-17's gunners claimed six fighters shot down, before the Fortress returned to its base. By 14 November, Ninth Air Force had B-17s at its disposal, sending a half dozen Fortresses to attack Bengasi's harbor, with only one of the B-17s locating and bombing the target. Two days later, 12th Air Force sent six B-17s from the 97th Bomb Group, which had moved to Algiers, to attack Sidi Ahmed airfield at Bizerte, to become the first 12th Air Force bomb group to fly a combat mission in Africa. On 19 November, B-17s of 12th Air Force enjoyed the protection of P-38 escort fighters when the bombers attacked El Aouina airfield. By 23 November, Eighth Air Force heavy bomber crews reported the change in Luftwaffe fighter tactics from stern

attacks to head-on passes, capitalizing on weak frontal firepower on both B-17s and B-24s, later to be remedied in part by the addition of chin turrets on B-17s and nose turrets on B-24s.[28]

The winter of 1942 in North Africa held surprises for American airmen, most of whom were there for the first time. The perception of blowing sands and arid lands gave way to winter rains that made quagmires of some landing fields. On 28 November, 12th AF sent 35 B-17s from the 97th and 301st Bomb Groups to attack the dock and airfield areas of Bizerte. Mud prevented launching P-38 escort fighters. Two of the Fortresses were lost to enemy fighters. Next day, in the tropics, Fifth Air Force B-17s encountered a Japanese force of four destroyers, loaded with troops from Rabaul, intended to reinforce Gona. The B-17s inflicted damage to two of the destroyers and prompted the others to retreat back through the Vitiaz Strait, site

of the action. In December, SOPAC B-17s bombed Munda 21 times to halt or at least slow construction of Japanese airfields there. The construction continued. December saw a continuation of pressure on repeat targets by B-17s around the world. As production increased, 12th Air Force was able to put up 36 B-17s against targets at Tunis and Bizerte on 17 December 1942.[29]

Col. Curtis LeMay, commander of the 305th Bomb Group of the Eighth Air Force, studied problems of bomber defense against fighter attacks in 1942. The best formation he devised for bringing maximum guns to bear on any attackers consisted of three-ship elements staggered in a squadron, with squadrons staggered in a group, to provide a tight box formation that could still maneuver. What this combat box gained in defensive protection it gave up in individual aircraft maneuvering capability, used by bombardiers and pilots to set up individual bomb runs.

LeMay's solution was to remove the obligation of bombing accuracy from each plane in the formation and place it with a lead bombardier, on whose signal the other planes in the compact box would release their bombs. If the lead bombardier was accurate, the rest of the box should achieve a tight pattern of coverage over the target area. LeMay put his idea into service on 30 December 1942 in a raid on the Lorient submarine pens. Not all went as well as it could; the bomb run into the sun gave Luftwaffe fighters an advantage in their head-on attacks, which cost one B-17 out of the 91st Bomb Group in the formation. After leaving the target, a B-17 from another group turned away from the formation, as one of LeMay's 305th BG Fortresses followed it to offer some additional firepower against the German fighters that ultimately downed both of the removed bombers. The lesson was clear: It was imperative to stick with the formation.[30]

The first Eighth AF mission of 1943 gave Colonel LeMay a chance to further prove his formation theory on 3 January. His 305th Bomb Group led 85 bombers to the flak-protected submarine facilities at St. Nazaire. To give the formation time to set up for good bombing results, a long straight run-in was made, with the bombers spaced from 20,000 to 22,000 feet in altitude. A gale force headwind stretched out the run-in time over the target, putting the B-17s at the mercy of heavy flak barrages for longer than usual. Of great concern was the evident improvement in German flak accuracy that day. Where previous missions had enjoyed relative immunity from flak above 20,000 feet, the

When two B-17s at Las Vegas Army Airfield collided on 9 March 1944, the result was a wrinkled wingtip and smashed Plexiglas and aluminum framing. Like another photo of Las Vegas B-17Gs, the aircraft with the damaged nose in this photo has only the righthand cheek gun installation. (Via Marty Isham)

Fortresses over St. Nazaire this day had to fly into the path of a predicted barrage, instead of being individually targeted by the gunners far below. Two Fortresses fell from flak, and a third missing B-17 was presumed to be a victim of the barrage. More than half the returning

First the prop dome comes off, followed by the propeller, before an engine can be changed on an Eighth Air Force B-17G. (USAF)

With its unit markings overpainted and its turrets removed, a Project Aphrodite B-17F was photographed on 9 November 1944. Aphrodite used aging Eighth Air Force B-17Fs loaded with high explosives, to be flown by remote control into fortified targets.

bombers had flak damage; daylight precision bombing would not be waged without costly challenges from the Germans. Four more Fortresses were downed by fighters that day. But the tight bombing pattern was seen as evidence supporting LeMay's premise. Bombing on the leader became a common practice in the Eighth Air Force.[31]

In mid-January 1943, when Allied ground advances toward the Japanese in the vicinity of Mount Austen outreached the ability of native carriers to keep the Allies supplied, 13th Air Force B-17s from Henderson Field airlifted ammunition, water, and rations to the troops, using improvised parachutes when not wrapping the supplies in canvas or burlap and

pushing them overboard. A Fortress from Alaska's 11th Air Force, upon the alleged sighting of a submarine on 30 January, dropped four depth charges and a bomb, after which a whale was seen to surface. B-17s in North Africa participated in the effort to hit Gen. Erwin Rommel's forces withdrawing toward Kasserine on 22 February 1943. The Fortresses from Northwest African Air Forces (NAAF) bombed Kasserine Pass while twin-engine B-25s hit a nearby bridge. Next day, the NAAF B-17s bombed Kairouan airfield and troops retreating through Kasserine Pass, repeating again on the 24th of the month. As 1943 unfolded, Eighth Air Force increasingly achieved adequate fighter escort for its heavy bomber missions, resulting typically in lower losses among the bombers. Thus, two major aspects of American strategic bombardment doctrine were codified by this time: Tight box formations, bombing on the lead bombardier's signal, and adequate fighter escort were vital to the success of daylight precision bombardment. The first concept could be implemented quickly; but fighter escort was limited by production capacity and the evolution of fighters with sufficient range to accompany the bombers to ever more distant targets deep in enemy territory.[32]

Project Aphrodite B-17F has wind deflector ahead of open crew hatch, to enable pilots to bail out after getting the explosive-laden Fortress airborne and handing it off to a director aircraft. For its one-way mission, the Fortress has been stripped of armament and even the ADF football antenna. Drop tank was part of smoke generator system to enable director, flying at a safe distance, to track path of Aphrodite toward target. This veteran B-17F carries three black crosses indicating victories over German fighters.

To help Eighth Air Force B-17Fs cope with head-on attacks, several field-modifications were instituted in England. The general premise was to put a flexible .50-caliber machine gun in the nose with a reasonable straight-ahead field of fire. This necessitated welding an internal tube structure to support the weight and recoil of the .50-caliber gun, which was more than the Plexiglas nose could sustain unaided. Sockets for .30-caliber machine guns recessed into B-17F Plexiglas nosepieces were virtually useless. Later versions of the F-model would use angled cheek gun windows which provided more forward fire than flat cheek windows in the nose of the first B-17Fs, but Fortress crews would have to wait for the introduction of the Bendix chin turret before they would have a truly viable frontal defensive armament.

The Battle of the Bismarck Sea began 2 March 1943 with Fifth Air Force B-17s and B-24s attacking a convoy of eight transports and eight destroyers steaming from Rabaul toward Huon Gulf. By the end of the day, the combined force of bombers had sunk or damaged four of the transports. During the first part of 1943, B-17s continued to be used singly and in small groups in the Pacific, often against shipping, and sometimes from strafing altitudes. On 4 May 1943, Eighth Air Force P-47 Thunderbolt fighters began giving escort for bombers up to 175 miles. This day, while the main targets for Eighth AF heavy bombers were the former Ford and General Motors factories in Antwerp, a luring group of more than 30 B-17s and B-24s aimed for the French coast, and successfully tied up about 100 German fighters — half the total number in the area

Head-on B-17F photo shows recess in top of nose for internally-braced .50-caliber machine gun, plus staggered cheek windows with guns pointing forward.

— and kept many of the fighters busy long enough to prevent their use against the main bomber force attacking Antwerp. The bomber build-up in England allowed four more B-17 groups, the 94th, 95th, 96th, and 351st, to be ready for combat by the 13th or 14th of May. Significant to the Air Force and to the evolution of B-17 operations, on 18 May, the Combined Bomber Offensive plan worked out between the USAAF and the RAF was approved by the Combined Chiefs of Staff. This provided for round-the-clock bombing, and gave Eighth Air Force the authorization it needed to proceed with daylight strategic precision bombing within the framework of the CBO. This represented a greater level of acceptance of daylight bombing doctrine than had been manifest before. Destruction of German fighters — control of the air — became the immediate priority, followed by German submarine facilities.[33]

YB-40 COMBAT DEBUT

On 29 May 1943, seven YB-40 escort fighter versions of the B-17

made their combat debut with an Eighth AF force hitting St. Nazaire. The heavy YB-40s proved unable to stay with the B-17s (especially as the bombers lightened their loads). Forcing the entire formation to slow down on the way home kept both protectors and the protected bombers over enemy territory longer than they would have wanted to be. Some ammunition feed problems also needed to be worked out. Ultimately, the use of heavy bombers as escorts would be abandoned before any similar YB-41 Liberator variants could reach combat, but not before at least one YB-40 would be lost on a combat mission to the Ruhr on 22 June.

A milestone in the maturation of heavy bombardment over Europe occurred on 28 July 1943 when P-47 Thunderbolt fighters used jettisonable belly tanks for the first time in combat, extending their escort range into Germany. As the B-17s returned from their target (an FW-190 factory at Oschersleben) they were picked up 30 miles deeper inside Germany than ever before by extended-range P-47s, surpris-

Pair of 15th Air Force B-17Gs in formation point out differences in early and late production. Swoose II (42-31844), foreground, is an early B-17G-BO (Boeing) product. It has the factory style tail gun emplacement and dark olive drab where cheek gun fittings and enclosed waist window covers with K-5 mounts were added. The waist windows on this old G-model are directly opposite each other, with the national insignia applied in front of the window on the fuselage. The silver Fortress (44-6406) is a B-17G-DL (Douglas) aircraft. It has the improved Cheyenne pumpkin tail turret and staggered waist windows with either K-6 or K-7 enclosed gun mounts. With the right waist window moved forward, the right fuselage insignia is moved aft. (Gerry Furney collection)

ing and destroying nine German fighters for the loss of one P-47. The Eighth Air Force marked its first anniversary of combat with a 17 August 1943 mission that split 315 B-17s between targeting ball bearing factories at Schweinfurt and a Messerschmitt complex at Regensburg. Substantial damage to the targets was logged, but the B-17s, unable to be escorted at their deepest penetration, fell prey to enduring fighter attacks. The Fortresses lost 60 of their number in that one combined mission — a staggering loss that could not be sustained for long. Clearly, the need for deeper escort by fighters was vital to the continued daylight precision bombing offensive over Germany.

Another element in the growing daylight bombing arsenal against Germany got its first large-scale operational utilization in the ETO on 27 September 1943 when H2S radar-equipped pathfinders led 244 other B-17s to bomb the port of Emden through cloud cover. Radar bombing through overcast (BTO) increased the number of days the bombers could attack German targets.

By early October 1943, B-17 bombing missions in the Pacific were infrequent and nearing an end, as B-24s swelled the Pacific ranks, with new production B-17s heading to Europe instead. Twelfth Air Force B-17s were putting pressure on Italian targets while Eighth AF Fortresses struck from the west. Eventually, 12th AF B-17s would migrate to the new 15th Air Force, which was activated on 1 November 1943.

SCHWEINFURT SLOWED FORTRESS OFFENSE

When 60 B-17s were downed by fighters while on a mission to bomb the German ball bearing industry at Schweinfurt on 14 October 1943, the magnitude of these losses caused a momentary lull in strategic bombing missions deep into Germany. Another key element in the daylight bombing regimen was still in development and not ready for service yet — when the P-51B Mustang reached England, escort would be available deeper into Germany. The Schweinfurt raid did considerable damage to the bearing industry, and prompted Germany to reorganize it. In the fall of 1943, Eighth Air Force B-17s and B-24s continued to expand their use of pathfinder radar-equipped aircraft for blind bombing raids; 12th AF and then 15th AF used its Fortresses to keep pressure on German transportation targets in Italy, including rail-yards and bridges. On 13 December 1943, with P-51 Mustangs escorting to the limit of their range, a mixed force totaling 649 B-17s and B-24s from Eighth AF bombed port areas at Bremen and Hamburg, and the U-boat yards at Kiel. In 1944, even greater range would be gained for the Mustang escorts. On 19 December, about 150 Fortresses from 15th Air Force attacked the Messerschmitt aircraft plant at Augsburg and marshaling yards at Innsbruck, Austria. On 20 December, Eighth AF logged its first use of window — aluminum strips dumped into the air to obscure the picture on German anti-aircraft radar scopes. This would be a useful tool for B-17s and B-24s in the continuing war of technology over Europe.[34]

Gunner peers from the open left waist window of a Second Bomb Group, 20th Bomb Squadron B-17 on 21 January 1944. Hastily brushed paint surrounds the national insignia, suggesting it had been bordered in red, and was covered over with new insignia blue or even black, judging from the disparity between the border and the blue field surrounding the star. This open waist mount is fitted with a Bell E-11 recoil adaptor instead of the different E-8 or E-12 styles.

Coiled springs balance the weight of a .50-caliber machine gun in a K-5 gun mount built into an early enclosed B-17G right waist window. SSgt. Stanley H. Katz of Brooklyn looks from the removable center window of this mud-spattered 15th Air Force Fortress of the Second Bomb Group at Amendola, Italy, in May 1944. (USAF)

Ball turrets on 15th Air Force B-17s were especially susceptible to muddy conditions at some Italian air bases. Gunner Donald E. Malcomson shows an early style turret with curved trunnion fairings, in May 1944.

In 15th Air Force on 10 January 1944, escorted B-17s bombed marshaling yards at Sofia. Attacked by about 60 fighters, the B-17s lost two of their force in a raging air battle, for which the Fortresses and their escort claimed 28 enemy aircraft shot down. In the midst of recurring bad flying weather, on 12 February B-17s and B-24s of 15th Air Force targeted troop concentrations and highways in the vicinity of Cecina as well as near Lake Nemi. Sometimes, the strategic bombers performed missions that appeared more tactical in nature. On 15 February, about 100 B-17s from 15th Air Force bombed the abbey at Monte Cassino. As if to emphasize strategic bombardment as the primary purpose for being in England, on 22 February 1944 Headquarters Eighth Air Force was redesignated Headquarters, U.S. Strategic Air Forces in Europe and Headquarters VIII Bomber Command was redesignated Headquarters Eighth Air Force.

On 4 March, 31 Eighth Air Force Fortresses from the 95th and 100th Bomb Groups bombed a target just southwest of Berlin, thereby becoming the first American bombers to strike the German capital vicinity.[35] Fourth Fighter Group P-51 Mustangs, enhanced with a fuselage gas tank as well as drop tanks, escorted them over Berlin. On 9 March, Berlin was visited by 300 B-17s from Eighth AF. As the early months of 1944 progressed, Eighth Air Force B-17s tended to target specific German industries and V-weapon sites, as their 15th Air Force counterparts went after transportation targets and provided bombing support for the Fifth Army. On 5 April 1944, a force of 334 B-17s and B-24s from 15th Air Force bombed Ploesti, Leskovac, and Nish. The downing of 39 Eighth Air Force B-17s and B-24s on 24 April occurred in spite of a large attack that day by 15th Air Force Fortresses and Liberators over Ploesti and Bucharest which drew many fighters away from the Eighth Air Force attack. On 29 April, when 579 Eighth Air Force B-17s and B-24s bombed Berlin, their crews estimated the number of opposing German fighters at a staggering 350 aircraft.

EMPHASIS ON AIRFIELDS FOR D-DAY

On 9 May, Eighth AF sent a total of 797 B-17s and B-24s to bomb German airfields in France, commencing an offensive intended to deny these assets to the Germans for the impending Allied invasion of the Continent, less than a month away. Meanwhile, 15th AF B-17s and B-24s continued to fly interdiction missions in support of ground forces. And pressure on Berlin was not relieved during this period, as 493 B-17s bombed the Friedrichstrasse portion of the German city on 19 May, as 49 other Eighth AF Fortresses attacked port facilities at Kiel. Again on 24 May, 447 B-17s from Eighth Air Force rumbled over Berlin while 72 others attacked targets of opportunity in the area. On the last day of May 1944, about 480 B-17s and B-24s from 15th Air Force bombed refineries and other targets in the Ploesti, Romania, area. On 2 June 1944, 15th Air Force sent 130 Fortresses with 70 escorting P-51s on the first shuttle-bombing mission cooperating with the Soviet Union. The B-17s bombed marshaling yards at Debreczen and landed in the Soviet Union at Poltava and Mirgorod. On 5 June, Eighth AF B-17s attacked French coastal targets, some of which were intended to throw off any German guesses about the location of a possible Allied invasion. Next day, when the invasion took place at Normandy, heavy bombers supported the effort. That day in the Soviet Union, 15th AF B-17s made another shuttle mission from Soviet fields, landing back in the USSR again.[36]

In the weeks following the Allied invasion of continental Europe, Eighth Air Force B-17s bombed German airfields in France to deny

the enemy airpower over the battlefield, while also targeting V-weapon sites and, later in the month of June, German oil production and storage capacity. On 21 June 1944, Eighth AF had a total of 145 B-17s over Germany, bound for that air force's first shuttle mission to Russia. Escort was provided all the way by P-47s that handed the duty off to shifts of P-51s, the last of which accompanied the B-17s to Russia. The primary target, a synthetic oil refinery at Ruhland, was hit by 123 of the B-17s; other targets were attacked by the remainder. About 50 miles southeast of Brest Litovsk, a force estimated at 20 to 30 fighters attacked the B-17s. During the mission, one B-17 was lost to unknown causes. Seventy-three Fortresses landed at Poltava, and 71 at Mirgorod. That night, German bombers, aided by flare-dropping aircraft, attacked the field at Poltava over a two-hour period, destroying 47 of the B-17s and damaging many of the others. Stored gasoline and ammunition also suffered in the Poltava attack. Next day, the unscathed B-17s at Mirgorod, and the escorting P-51s from Piryatin, moved farther east into the Soviet Union for safety. There followed several days in Russia while the usable Fortresses were readied for the return shuttle mission and moved to Poltava on 25 June, only to return to their eastern strips when weather canceled the mission. Finally, on 26 June, 72 B-17s took off from Poltava and Mirgorod, made rendezvous with 55 P-51s from Piryatin, and bombed an oil refinery and marshaling yard at Drohobycz. One Fortress returned to the USSR with mechanical problems while the balance proceeded to Foggia, Italy, and then on to England in subsequent days. As the Poltava-to-Foggia shuttle was taking place, 15th AF B-17s and B-24s totaling 677 bombers attacked targets in the vicinity of Vienna.[37]

Fifteenth Air Force's first Pathfinder-led mission was a 9 July 1944 effort sending 222 B-17s and B-24s to bomb the Xenia and Concordia Vega oil refineries at Ploesti. On 14 July, a force of 319 B-17s from Eighth Air Force airdropped supplies to French interior forces in southern France. The magnitude of Eighth Air Force B-17 operations by this time in the war was evidenced on 28 July when 653 B-17s were mustered to bomb a synthetic oil plant at Merseburg, while 57 more B-17s attacked an aircraft engine factory at Taucha and the Wiesbaden marshaling yards, for a total Eighth Air Force B-17 effort of 710 Flying Fortresses. Seven B-17s were lost by Eighth AF that day. Next day, an even greater effort by Eighth AF logged 1,044 B-17s pitted against several targets, demonstrating the Eighth's ability to sustain high levels of Fortress operations on two consecutive days — a far cry from the early sorties of 1942.

On 14 August, to support the invasion fleet heading toward southern France, B-17s and B-24s from 15th Air Force bombed gun positions in the vicinities of Genoa and Toulon. On the 15th of the month, Fortresses and Liberators from 15th AF conducted that air force's first heavy bomber mass night raid, pounding the beaches in the area around Cannes-Toulon immediately prior to the invasion there by Allied troops. Next day, 108 B-17s from 15th AF, supporting Operation Dragoon, as the invasion of southern France was known, attacked railroad bridges at several locations including Grenoble. During several months of 1944, B-17s repeatedly bombed oil refineries at Ploesti from high altitude. On 17 September 1944, two 15th Air Force B-17s with an escort of 41 Mustangs evacuated wounded airmen from Czechoslovakia to Italy. The pace of the war was relentless, pausing only reluctantly for weather, and occasionally to regenerate forces after a period of sustained

Later style ball turrets deleted curved side fairings, exposing the trunnions directly. This oil- and mud-spattered example was on a 15th Air Force Fortress in Italy in 1944. (USAF)

Shuttle missions to the Soviet Union included the peril of nocturnal raids by German bombers that charred this B-17G-DL and left its ball turret column pointing out of the wreckage like a sign post. (USAF)

operations. On 23 October 1944, a mix of about 500 B-17s and B-24s from 15th Air Force rained bombs on a list of targets ranging from Germany and Czechoslovakia to northern Italy. On 3 November, 15th AF tried a technique designed to permit operations in bad weather: Flying without escort, a mixture of 46 B-17s and B-24s bombed several different targets in individual aircraft attacks instead of formation bombing. The Fortresses and Liberators used cloud cover for protection. In a turnabout of the usual scenario, more than 30 other heavy bombers sent out that day on this single-ship plan had to abort when the weather cleared![38]

Forsaking the stereotypical daylight attack, on 7 December 1944, 31 B-17s and B-24s from 15th Air Force staged pre-dawn raids on marshaling yards at Klagenfurt, Salzburg, Villach, and Lienz, as well as communications targets at Mittersill, Wolfsberg, Spittal an der Drau, Sankt Veit in Defereggen, and Trieste. Next day, two dozen Fortresses and Liberators from 15th AF again executed several predawn

attacks, including the oil refinery at Moosbierbaum. The lessons learned in unescorted B-17 missions prompted more than 200 Eighth Air Force B-17s to be recalled from missions to German targets on 13 December when weather grounded their intended fighter escort. On 24 December 1944, Eighth Air Force dispatched more than 2,000 heavy bombers, nearly 1,900 of which attacked 11 airfields and more than 70 other targets. A healthy percentage of these bombers were B-17s. When heavy overcast threatened the safety of more than 100 Eighth AF B-17s following an attack on the marshaling yards at Kaiserslautern on 18 January 1945, most of the Fortresses were diverted to land at airfields on continental Europe. Occasionally in the early months of 1945, a few 15th Air Force B-17s joined a slightly larger number of B-24s on supply drop missions to partisans in northern Italy and Yugoslavia. A foray by 109 Fortresses from 15th AF to bomb a Ruhland oil refinery on 15 March 1945 was the 15th AF's deepest incursion into Germany, while 103 other 15th

AF B-17s bombed an alternate targeted refinery at Kolin.[39] Fifteenth Air Force also reached Berlin, as on 24 March when a force of more than 150 B-17s set out to bomb a tank works there. Flak and Me-262 jets plucked several Fortresses from the operation; defending the B-17s were Mustangs, engaging the German jets when possible and downing several. Fortress gunners also claimed several Me-262s that day.[40] The 15th Air Force was close to finishing its wartime strategic bombardment career; attacks on transportation and other tactical targets to support Allied ground operations continued until 1 May 1945 when 27 B-17s bombed marshaling yards at Salzburg on what became 15th Air Force's last bombing mission of World War Two.

In March 1945, the Eighth Air Force's Fifth Emergency Rescue Squadron (ERS) began supplanting its OA-10A Catalinas with a lifeboat-dropping converted B-17G from the 457th Bomb Group. The first use of this boat-dropping technique by a U.S. aircraft was logged on 31 March 1945 near Denmark.[41]

Eighth Air Force tried dropping napalm canisters from heavy bombers, including a contingent of B-17s, on 15 April 1945. Targets were German ground installations including gun emplacements, pillboxes, and tank trenches. Negligible effect prompted Eighth AF headquarters to recommend discontinuing its use against this type of target. Eighth Air Force's last heavy bomber mission against an industrial target came on 25 April 1945 when a force of about 275 B-17s, escorted by P-51s, bombed the Plzen-Skoda armament works and an airfield in Czechoslovakia.

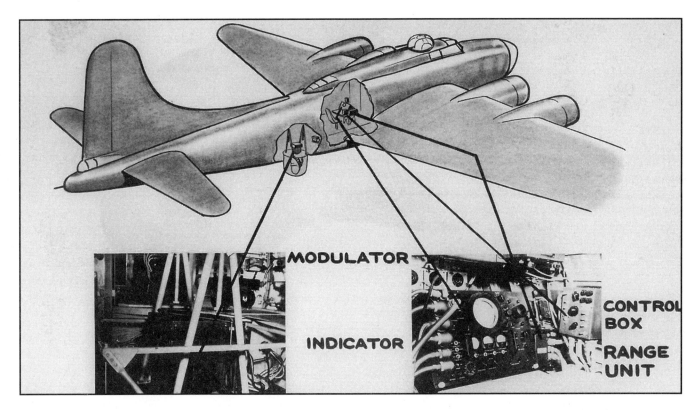

Cutaway drawing shows H2X radar unit and operator's station in a B-17. (Air Force)

Two days later, Eighth Air Force reverted to its original, and smaller, size authorization of 48 aircraft per bomb group, down from 68; the flow to Eighth AF of replacement B-17s had also stopped by then. On 1 May, nearly 400 Eighth Air Force B-17s dropped emergency food supplies in The Hague and the vicinity of Rotterdam. Next day, and again on 3, 5, 6, and 7 May, B-17s dropped more food supplies in populated areas of the Netherlands in a remarkable effort to save civilians from starvation in war-ravaged areas, with German gunners agreeing to keep their weapons silent during these humanitarian air-drops. Meanwhile, on 7 May the German High Command surrendered unconditionally, to be effective 9 May 1945.[42]

A few other B-17s saw miscellaneous service in the Pacific in 1945 as officer transportation and SB-17 lifeboat-dropping rescue aircraft, but combat for USAAF B-17s ended with the fall of Germany.

[1] *Army Air Forces Statistical Digest, World War II*, Office of Statistical Control, HQ, USAAF, December 1945. [2] *Ibid.* [3] *Ibid.* [4] *Ibid.* [5] *Ibid.* [6] *Ibid.* [7] Report No. E-54, "B-17 and B-24 Crews: A Comparison — Based on answers of 3000 officers and men in heavy bomber crews in the Eighth U.S. Air Force to an anonymous questionnaire completed during the week 28 May - 5 June, 1944" by Research Branch, Special Service Division, Headquarters, European Theater of Operations, July 1944. (AFHRA) [8] *Ibid.* [9] *Ibid.* [10] Report No. E-52, "Difficulty of Missions — Including statistics provided by Statistical Control Section, Eighth Air Force — A Supplement to: 'Survey of Heavy Bombardment Groups in ETO — A Preliminary Report based on answers of 3000 officers and men in heavy bomber crews in the Eighth U.S. Air Force to an anonymous questionnaire completed during the week 28 May - 5 June, 1944'", by Research Branch, Special Service Division, Headquarters, European Theater of Operations, June 1944. (AFHRA) [11] Kit C. Carter and Robert Mueller, compilers, *Combat Chronology, 1941-1945, U.S. Army Air Forces in World War II*, Center for Air Force History, Washington, D.C., 1991. [12] *Ibid.* [13] Excerpted from handwritten log found in one of the evacuation aircraft, and kept in the Air Force Historical Research Agency, Maxwell AFB, Alabama. [14] Kit C. Carter and Robert Mueller, compilers, *Combat Chronology, 1941-1945, U.S. Army Air Forces in World War II*, Center for Air Force History, Washington, D.C., 1991. [15] *Ibid.* [16] *Ibid.* [17] Excerpted from an unpublished manuscript written by the author, and incorporating an interview with Maj. Gen. Brooke E. Allen, USAF (Retired), circa 1977. [18] *Ibid.* [19] Kit C. Carter and Robert Mueller, compilers, *Combat Chronology, 1941-1945, U.S. Army Air Forces in World War II*, Center for Air Force History, Washington, D.C., 1991. [20] *Ibid.* [21] *Ibid.* [22] *Ibid.* [23] *Ibid.* [24] Steve Birdsall, *Flying Buccaneers — The Illustrated Story of Kenney's Fifth Air Force*, Doubleday, Garden City, NY, 1977. [25] Kit C. Carter and Robert Mueller, compilers, *Combat Chronology, 1941-1945, U.S. Army Air Forces in World War II*, Center for Air Force History, Washington, D.C., 1991. [26] Roger A. Freeman, *The Mighty Eighth — A History of the U.S. 8th Army Air Force*, Doubleday, Garden City, NY, 1970. [27] Kit C. Carter and Robert Mueller, compilers, *Combat Chronology, 1941-1945, U.S. Army Air Forces in World War II*, Center for Air Force History, Washington, D.C., 1991. [28] *Ibid.* [29] *Ibid.* [30] Roger A. Freeman, *The Mighty Eighth — A History of the U.S. 8th Army Air Force*, Doubleday, Garden City, NY, 1970. [31] *Ibid.* [32] Kit C. Carter and Robert Mueller, compilers, *Combat Chronology, 1941-1945, U.S. Army Air Forces in World War II*, Center for Air Force History, Washington, D.C., 1991. [33] *Ibid.* [34] *Ibid.* [35] Kenn C. Rust, *Eighth Air Force Story*, Historical Aviation Album, Temple City, Calif., 1978. [36] Kit C. Carter and Robert Mueller, compilers, *Combat Chronology, 1941-1945, U.S. Army Air Forces in World War II*, Center for Air Force History, Washington, D.C., 1991. [37] *Ibid.* [38] *Ibid.* [39] *Ibid.* [40] Kenn C. Rust, *Fifteenth Air Force Story*, Historical Aviation Album, Temple City, Calif., 1976. [41] Roger A. Freeman, *The Mighty Eighth — A History of the U.S. 8th Army Air Force*, Doubleday, Garden City, NY, 1970. [42] Kit C. Carter and Robert Mueller, compilers, *Combat Chronology, 1941-1945, U.S. Army Air Forces in World War II*, Center for Air Force History, Washington, D.C., 1991.

TESTS AND 4 PROPOSALS

EVALUATING WAYS TO IMPROVE THE B-17

American faith in heavy bombardment may have blinded designers and the Air Corps to the dangers posed by ever more capable fighters. Clearly, the pre-war B-17 was insufficient to ward off fighter attacks, as the British quickly learned with the Fortress I variants they sent against German targets in Germany and Norway in 1941. But defensive upgrades were already in the works, their value only underscored by the early British experience with Fortress Is. In fact, when the United States furnished B-17Cs to the British to become Fortress Is, it was with the recommendation that they not be employed in a hostile combat environment. Before the entry of the United States into the war, American Air Force observers

in Great Britain were not furnished much information about British power turrets. This curious withholding of information between friendly nations probably only served to accelerate American turret designs. The first major revision to the Fortress line came with the 1941 introduction of the B-17E, using, for the first time, power turrets designed by Sperry and Bendix for the upper and lower positions, respectively.

The AAF Proving Ground Command, established at Eglin Field, Florida, on 1 April 1942, quickly set to work evaluating armaments and suitability of AAF aircraft including the B-17 Flying Fortress. By that time, the B-17E was in service. Nonetheless, a prewar B-17C, num-

ber 40-2046, arrived at Eglin from Wright Field, Ohio, on 16 May 1942, sporting a Sperry central fire control system and two 20MM cannons in the nose. Tests were conducted on this armament system, not with intent of deploying it in aging B-17Cs, but for its potential in other aircraft, especially the B-29 Superfortress. The Sperry system in the B-17C was compared with an experimental General Electric central fire control system mounted in an outdated B-24C Liberator. The Sperry system was shown to be more accurate, but the General Electric equipment was said to be "functionally more reliable." However, an AAF report said: "Neither the B-24 nor the B-17 was regarded as a sufficiently stable firing platform for the accurate operation of a central fire control system."[1]

The 20MM cannons in the nose of the B-17C were mounted at about floor level. Testers at Eglin investigated the ability of this installation to fire effectively at an aircraft making head-on attacks. An AAF report said: "The B-17C was restricted to maneuvers that could be performed within a three-airplane formation. On this basis it was impossible to hold an attacking airplane within the sights of the cannon long enough to fire effectively. The B-17C could not

3/4 FRONT VIEW - TAIL TURRET ASSY CHANGE BEGINS ON SHIP #101

Early factory style B-17E tail gun emplacement was contained in a fuselage end cap that could be attached as a unit. (Peter M. Bowers collection)

TESTS AND 4 PROPOSALS

EVALUATING WAYS TO IMPROVE THE B-17

American faith in heavy bombardment may have blinded designers and the Air Corps to the dangers posed by ever more capable fighters. Clearly, the pre-war B-17 was insufficient to ward off fighter attacks, as the British quickly learned with the Fortress I variants they sent against German targets in Germany and Norway in 1941. But defensive upgrades were already in the works, their value only underscored by the early British experience with Fortress Is. In fact, when the United States furnished B-17Cs to the British to become Fortress Is, it was with the recommendation that they not be employed in a hostile combat environment. Before the entry of the United States into the war, American Air Force observers

in Great Britain were not furnished much information about British power turrets. This curious withholding of information between friendly nations probably only served to accelerate American turret designs. The first major revision to the Fortress line came with the 1941 introduction of the B-17E, using, for the first time, power turrets designed by Sperry and Bendix for the upper and lower positions, respectively.

The AAF Proving Ground Command, established at Eglin Field, Florida, on 1 April 1942, quickly set to work evaluating armaments and suitability of AAF aircraft including the B-17 Flying Fortress. By that time, the B-17E was in service. Nonetheless, a prewar B-17C, num-

ber 40-2046, arrived at Eglin from Wright Field, Ohio, on 16 May 1942, sporting a Sperry central fire control system and two 20MM cannons in the nose. Tests were conducted on this armament system, not with intent of deploying it in aging B-17Cs, but for its potential in other aircraft, especially the B-29 Superfortress. The Sperry system in the B-17C was compared with an experimental General Electric central fire control system mounted in an outdated B-24C Liberator. The Sperry system was shown to be more accurate, but the General Electric equipment was said to be "functionally more reliable." However, an AAF report said: "Neither the B-24 nor the B-17 was regarded as a sufficiently stable firing platform for the accurate operation of a central fire control system."[1]

The 20MM cannons in the nose of the B-17C were mounted at about floor level. Testers at Eglin investigated the ability of this installation to fire effectively at an aircraft making head-on attacks. An AAF report said: "The B-17C was restricted to maneuvers that could be performed within a three-airplane formation. On this basis it was impossible to hold an attacking airplane within the sights of the cannon long enough to fire effectively. The B-17C could not

3/4 FRONT VIEW-TAIL TURRET ASSY CHANGE BEGINS ON SHIP #101

Early factory style B-17E tail gun emplacement was contained in a fuselage end cap that could be attached as a unit. (Peter M. Bowers collection)

WARBIRDTECH
SERIES

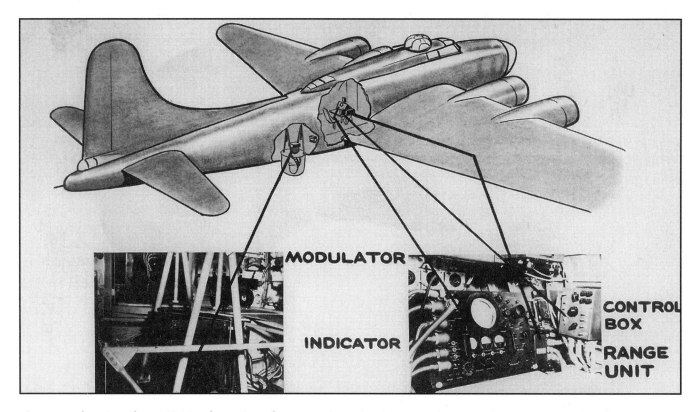

Cutaway drawing shows H2X radar unit and operator's station in a B-17. (Air Force)

Two days later, Eighth Air Force reverted to its original, and smaller, size authorization of 48 aircraft per bomb group, down from 68; the flow to Eighth AF of replacement B-17s had also stopped by then. On 1 May, nearly 400 Eighth Air Force B-17s dropped emergency food supplies in The Hague and the vicinity of Rotterdam. Next day, and again on 3, 5, 6, and 7 May, B-17s dropped more food supplies in populated areas of the Netherlands in a remarkable effort to save civilians from starvation in war-ravaged areas, with German gunners agreeing to keep their weapons silent during these humanitarian airdrops. Meanwhile, on 7 May the German High Command surrendered unconditionally, to be effective 9 May 1945.[42]

A few other B-17s saw miscellaneous service in the Pacific in 1945 as officer transportation and SB-17 lifeboat-dropping rescue aircraft, but combat for USAAF B-17s ended with the fall of Germany.

[1] *Army Air Forces Statistical Digest, World War II*, Office of Statistical Control, HQ, USAAF, December 1945. [2] *Ibid.* [3] *Ibid.* [4] *Ibid.* [5] *Ibid.* [6] *Ibid.* [7] Report No. E-54, "B-17 and B-24 Crews: A Comparison — Based on answers of 3000 officers and men in heavy bomber crews in the Eighth U.S. Air Force to an anonymous questionnaire completed during the week 28 May - 5 June, 1944" by Research Branch, Special Service Division, Headquarters, European Theater of Operations, July 1944. (AFHRA) [8] *Ibid.* [9] *Ibid.* [10] Report No. E-52, "Difficulty of Missions — Including statistics provided by Statistical Control Section, Eighth Air Force — A Supplement to: 'Survey of Heavy Bombardment Groups in ETO — A Preliminary Report based on answers of 3000 officers and men in heavy bomber crews in the Eighth U.S. Air Force to an anonymous questionnaire completed during the week 28 May - 5 June, 1944'", by Research Branch, Special Service Division, Headquarters, European Theater of Operations, June 1944. (AFHRA) [11] Kit C. Carter and Robert Mueller, compilers, *Combat Chronology, 1941-1945, U.S. Army Air Forces in World War II*, Center for Air Force History, Washington, D.C., 1991. [12] *Ibid.* [13] Excerpted from handwritten log found in one of the evacuation aircraft, and kept in the Air Force Historical Research Agency, Maxwell AFB, Alabama. [14] Kit C. Carter and Robert Mueller, compilers, *Combat Chronology, 1941-1945, U.S. Army Air Forces in World War II*, Center for Air Force History, Washington, D.C., 1991. [15] *Ibid.* [16] *Ibid.* [17] Excerpted from an unpublished manuscript written by the author, and incorporating an interview with Maj. Gen. Brooke E. Allen, USAF (Retired), circa 1977. [18] *Ibid.* [19] Kit C. Carter and Robert Mueller, compilers, *Combat Chronology, 1941-1945, U.S. Army Air Forces in World War II*, Center for Air Force History, Washington, D.C., 1991. [20] *Ibid.* [21] *Ibid.* [22] *Ibid.* [23] *Ibid.* [24] Steve Birdsall, *Flying Buccaneers — The Illustrated Story of Kenney's Fifth Air Force*, Doubleday, Garden City, NY, 1977. [25] Kit C. Carter and Robert Mueller, compilers, *Combat Chronology, 1941-1945, U.S. Army Air Forces in World War II*, Center for Air Force History, Washington, D.C., 1991. [26] Roger A. Freeman, *The Mighty Eighth — A History of the U.S. 8th Army Air Force*, Doubleday, Garden City, NY, 1970. [27] Kit C. Carter and Robert Mueller, compilers, *Combat Chronology, 1941-1945, U.S. Army Air Forces in World War II*, Center for Air Force History, Washington, D.C., 1991. [28] *Ibid.* [29] *Ibid.* [30] Roger A. Freeman, *The Mighty Eighth — A History of the U.S. 8th Army Air Force*, Doubleday, Garden City, NY, 1970. [31] *Ibid.* [32] Kit C. Carter and Robert Mueller, compilers, *Combat Chronology, 1941-1945, U.S. Army Air Forces in World War II*, Center for Air Force History, Washington, D.C., 1991. [33] *Ibid.* [34] *Ibid.* [35] Kenn C. Rust, *Eighth Air Force Story*, Historical Aviation Album, Temple City, Calif., 1978. [36] Kit C. Carter and Robert Mueller, compilers, *Combat Chronology, 1941-1945, U.S. Army Air Forces in World War II*, Center for Air Force History, Washington, D.C., 1991. [37] *Ibid.* [38] *Ibid.* [39] *Ibid.* [40] Kenn C. Rust, *Fifteenth Air Force Story*, Historical Aviation Album, Temple City, Calif., 1976. [41] Roger A. Freeman, *The Mighty Eighth — A History of the U.S. 8th Army Air Force*, Doubleday, Garden City, NY, 1970. [42] Kit C. Carter and Robert Mueller, compilers, *Combat Chronology, 1941-1945, U.S. Army Air Forces in World War II*, Center for Air Force History, Washington, D.C., 1991.

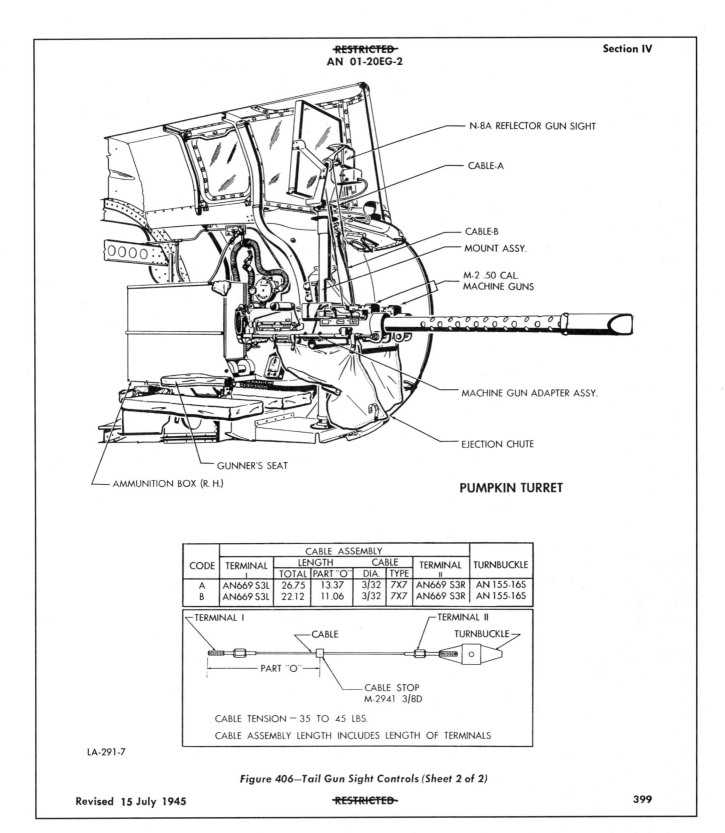

N-8A REFLECTOR GUN SIGHT

CABLE-A

CABLE-B

MOUNT ASSY.

M-2 .50 CAL.
MACHINE GUNS

MACHINE GUN ADAPTER ASSY.

EJECTION CHUTE

GUNNER'S SEAT

AMMUNITION BOX (R. H.)

PUMPKIN TURRET

CODE	TERMINAL I	CABLE ASSEMBLY				TERMINAL II	TURNBUCKLE
		LENGTH		CABLE			
		TOTAL	PART "O"	DIA.	TYPE		
A	AN669 S3L	26.75	13.37	3/32	7X7	AN669 S3R	AN 155-16S
B	AN669 S3L	22.12	11.06	3/32	7X7	AN669 S3R	AN 155-16S

TERMINAL I

CABLE

TERMINAL II

TURNBUCKLE

PART "O"

CABLE STOP
M-2941 3/8D

CABLE TENSION — 35 TO 45 LBS.

CABLE ASSEMBLY LENGTH INCLUDES LENGTH OF TERMINALS

LA-291-7

Figure 406—Tail Gun Sight Controls (Sheet 2 of 2)

The ultimate B-17 tail armament was the Cheyenne "pumpkin" turret, named for the United Airlines B-17 modification center at Cheyenne, Wyoming (and, presumably, for its rounded pumpkin-like shape). Enhanced visibility and range of motion were assets of this device over earlier Fortress tail gun emplacements. Some B-17Gs built with the older style tail gun unit had the Cheyenne model installed as a modification. Cheyenne tail guns used electrical N-8A reflector gunsight instead of ring-and-bead sight. Adjacent to gunsight in drawing is armor glass panel to protect gunner. (Don Keller/Air Depot)

A canvas boot provided some weather protection on the old-style B-17 tail gun emplacement. (USAF)

be effectively maneuvered against an airplane attacking from the front. It was recommended that flexible guns or a .50-caliber turret be installed on the B-17 for protection against nose attacks."[2] Even at this stage of development, before B-17s of the Eighth Air Force had faced the Luftwaffe, testers at Eglin were calling for increased frontal firepower for the B-17. The first attempts — .50-caliber machine guns in flush cheek windows — would prove insufficient by themselves.

An evaluation of B-17E armaments in the first four months of 1942 prompted the recommendation that the dome for the Sperry top turret, at that time a heavily-ribbed structure, be replaced by a bubble of "solid Plexiglas with no braces." (During production of B-17Fs and G-models, the *(text continued on page 70)*

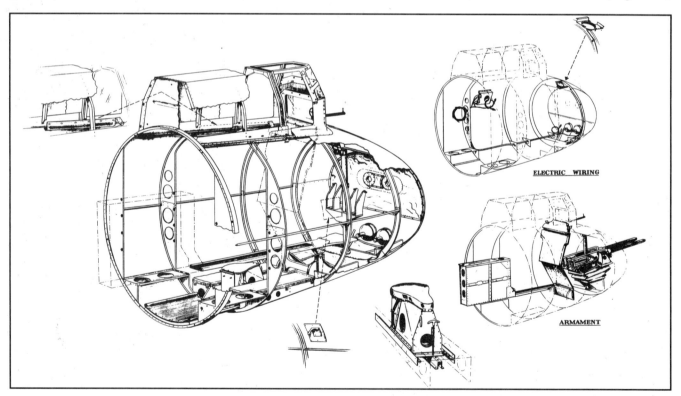

ELECTRIC WIRING

ARMAMENT

Views of factory-style tail gun compartment show armor plate protecting gunner's body, although his arms extended beyond to grasp guns.

B-17 WARPAINT

THE FLYING FORTRESS IN LIVING COLOR

The B-17 went from a slick silver speedster of the late 1930s to a somber camouflaged warrior in the darkest days of World War Two, only to emerge in natural metal again in late 1943, reaching England that way early in 1944. Only B-17Gs of the wartime variants were produced in natural metal finish; a scant handful of non-combatant earlier B-17s were stripped of their paint as well.

Aluminum B-17s could reflect light harshly into the faces of crewmen, with the effect aggravated by altitude. Even the original factory tail gun emplacement on silver B-17Gs received an anti-glare panel

Carrying external bomb racks, a factory-fresh B-17F passes Mount Rainier in western Washington. (Boeing)

Boeing workers detail a B-17C in 1940. Better mass-production capabilities were evolved later for wartime Fortress needs. (Boeing)

Eighth Air Force's D-Day Doll, *from the 447th Bomb Group, sits on a flak vest while donning a flak helmet. Chin turret fairing is painted red on this B-17G. (Al Lloyd collection)*

to aid the gunner, as did the portions of the engine nacelles facing the fuselage, and the nose ahead of the windscreen.

An unusual aspect of camouflaged B-17s was the use of olive drab as a ring around the engine nacelle lip. The underside gray paint did not intrude into this ring,

as it typically did on other camouflaged USAAF aircraft. This nuance of B-17 camouflage is often lost in postwar restoration jobs.

Blonde Bomber II used late-style nosepiece; anti-glare panel shows signs of fading on this 447th Bomb Group B-17G. (Al Lloyd collection)

In mid-May 1987, the restored B-17F Memphis Belle was readied fro a 17 May dedication ceremony in Memphis, Tennessee. Phil Starcer, nephew of the Belle's original decorator Tony Starcer, re-applied the pin-up art on the restored Fortress in Memphis. (Frederick A. Johnsen)

High demand for Flying Fortresses saw the USAAF keep some new B-17Es that had already been painted for the RAF, like the example nearest the camera, circa early 1942. (Boeing)

WARBIRD**TECH**
S E R I E S

A posed Boeing publicity Kodachrome shows Five Grand *before its name was added to the nose. Cheek window casting appears to be painted with light yellow zinc chromate primer; it probably was overpainted in aluminum silver before delivery to the USAAF.*

Even the ball turret and K-6 waist gun mount on Five Grand *were adorned with the signatures of Boeing workers when the aircraft was built in 1944.* (Boeing)

One of the last Fortresses in the U.S. Air Force (44-83885) was photographed at Patrick AFB, Florida, 21 May 1960. (Mal Holcomb)

SB-17G 44-83722 hung together by a thread after being parked at Yucca Flats, Nevada, for damage assessment in nuclear blast tests in the early 1950s. The forward fuselage was saved, and is in storage awaiting possible use in a restoration as of this writing. (National Archives)

Weapons no more, rows of B-17s awaited scrapping at Kingman, Arizona, circa 1947. Colorful tail markings indicate a large number of these aircraft returned from Eighth Air Force combat service. (Beall Masterson via Jeff Ethell)

Two Fortresses and a Liberator pass a Spanish-built Heinkel He-111 bomber during the 1978 Confederate Air Force warbird show in Harlingen, Texas. Units within the Confederate Air Force maintain two flyable B-17Gs, nicknamed Texas Raiders and Sentimental Journey. (Frederick A. Johnsen)

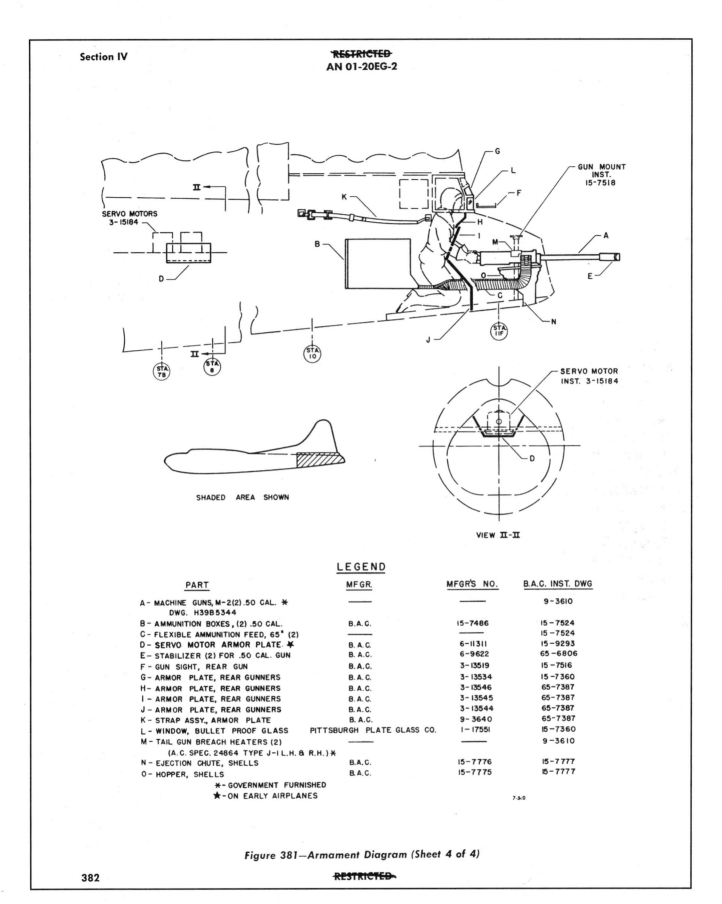

LEGEND

PART	MFGR.	MFGR'S NO.	B.A.C. INST. DWG
A – MACHINE GUNS, M-2(2) .50 CAL. ✱ DWG. H39B5344	—	—	9-3610
B – AMMUNITION BOXES, (2) .50 CAL.	B.A.C.	15-7486	15-7524
C – FLEXIBLE AMMUNITION FEED, 65° (2)	—	—	15-7524
D – SERVO MOTOR ARMOR PLATE. ✱	B.A.C.	6-11311	15-9293
E – STABILIZER (2) FOR .50 CAL. GUN	B.A.C.	6-9622	65-6806
F – GUN SIGHT, REAR GUN	B.A.C.	3-13519	15-7516
G – ARMOR PLATE, REAR GUNNERS	B.A.C.	3-13534	15-7360
H – ARMOR PLATE, REAR GUNNERS	B.A.C.	3-13546	65-7387
I – ARMOR PLATE, REAR GUNNERS	B.A.C.	3-13545	65-7387
J – ARMOR PLATE, REAR GUNNERS	B.A.C.	3-13544	65-7387
K – STRAP ASSY., ARMOR PLATE	B.A.C.	9-3640	65-7387
L – WINDOW, BULLET PROOF GLASS	PITTSBURGH PLATE GLASS CO.	1-17551	15-7360
M – TAIL GUN BREACH HEATERS (2) (A.C. SPEC. 24864 TYPE J-1 L.H. & R.H.) ✱	—	—	9-3610
N – EJECTION CHUTE, SHELLS	B.A.C.	15-7776	15-7777
O – HOPPER, SHELLS	B.A.C.	15-7775	15-7777

✱ – GOVERNMENT FURNISHED
★ – ON EARLY AIRPLANES

7-3-10

Figure 381—Armament Diagram (Sheet 4 of 4)

Original factory-style B-17 tail gun emplacement was used on B-17Es, Fs, and some Gs. Armor plate and an armored glass window afforded protection from rear attacks by fighters. (Don Keller/Air Depot)

Blister on the side of the tail gun compartment of B-17E 41-2539 accommodated refueling receiver line. During tests in 1943 with a B-24 modified as a tanker, 1,450 gallons of gas were transferred from the Liberator to the Fortress in 13-1/2 minutes over Florida. A mirror mounted to the tail guns at an angle allowed observation of refueling operations. (See also Consolidated B-24 Liberator, Warbird Tech Series Vol. 1, pp. 42-45.)

Hydraulic hauling winch mounted near tailwheel of B-17E 41-2539 for refueling tests reeled tanker hose aboard. (USAF)

(text continued from page 64) bracing became increasingly less obtrusive, but never went away entirely.) Since this was the first version of the B-17 to use a manned Sperry lower ball turret, the AAF noted: "The lower turret was so small that it was necessary to use men of the smallest stature to operate it." Significantly, the evaluators in early 1942 recognized the insufficiency of the single .30-caliber machine gun provided in the bombardier's compartment in the nose: "The Plexiglas windows were cracked by recoil. It was very difficult to aim the gun from the front upper socket, and very slow to change the gun from one socket to another. It was recommended that at least three .30 caliber guns be kept in position in the bombardier's compartment, if .30-caliber guns are retained, but that a study be made of the possibility of substituting one or two .50 caliber guns for the .30-caliber gun installation."[3] Ultimately, .50-caliber machine guns were

B-17E 41-9112 incorporated B-24 turrets in the tail and nose, a Martin upper turret, and a remotely-operated radio room gun. (Bowers collection)

FUSELAGE

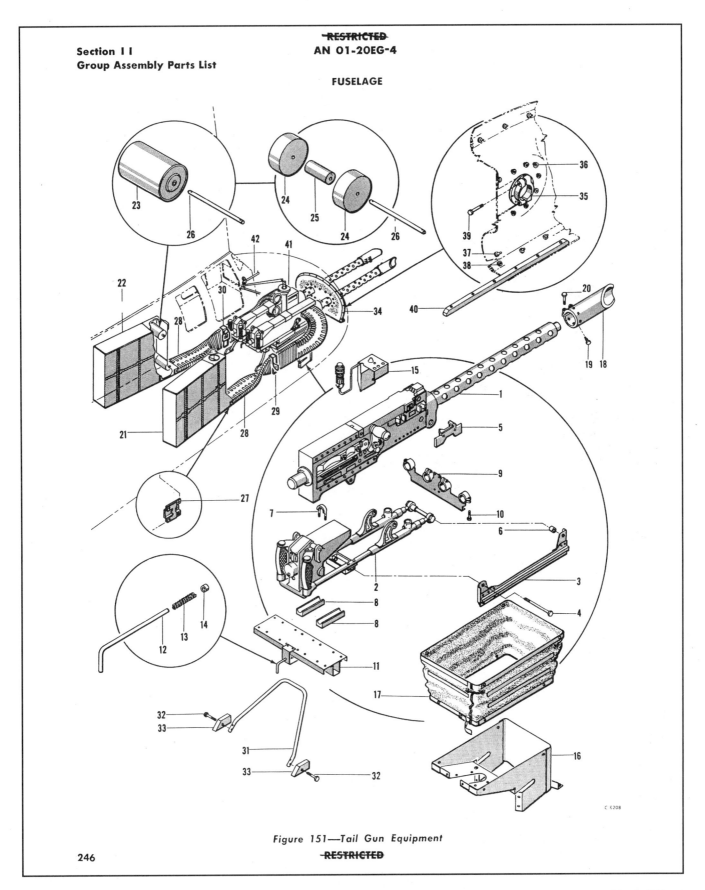

Figure 151—Tail Gun Equipment
~~RESTRICTED~~

246

B-17 tail guns used muzzle blast compensators with beveled openings (part 18). Guns were mounted in Bell E-11 recoil adaptors. Two large ammunition boxes fed the guns, as depicted in the B-17G illustrated parts manual.

Early B-17G underwent cold-soaking tests in Alaska. (Jim Morrow collection)

B-17F 42-29729 sported a B-32 nose turret and a recessed bombardier's station beneath the fuselage at the cockpit region. (Air Force photo via Peter M. Bowers collection)

installed in braced nose sockets in many B-17Fs, and evolutions of cheek gun windows mounting .50-calibers gave these side nose guns more frontal coverage as their mounting windows were altered to protrude slightly into the slipstream.

More radical was the modified B-17E (41-9112) brought to Wright Field from Eighth Air Force, sporting Consolidated B-24 tail turrets in the nose and tail. A Martin upper turret replaced the Sperry upper standard on B-17s; the ball turret was modified for better performance, and a remotely-controlled semi-turret was fitted in the radio compartment. Checked out in 1943, the unorthodox B-17E's Liberator nose and tail turrets performed satisfactorily, but the B-17G, with its chin turret and bulging cheek guns, was already in work, and other arrangements were envisioned for the tail guns. However, in the event these armaments did not pan out, testers recommended that the Consolidated tail turret be considered for installation in the nose and tail of production B-17s. The Martin upper turret passed its exam in

Its guns pointed at the camera, the A-16 chin turret provided a formidable frontal defense for the B-17G. Canvas zippered wind baffles enclosed the gun slots; metal baffles were developed later. (SDAM)

FUSELAGE

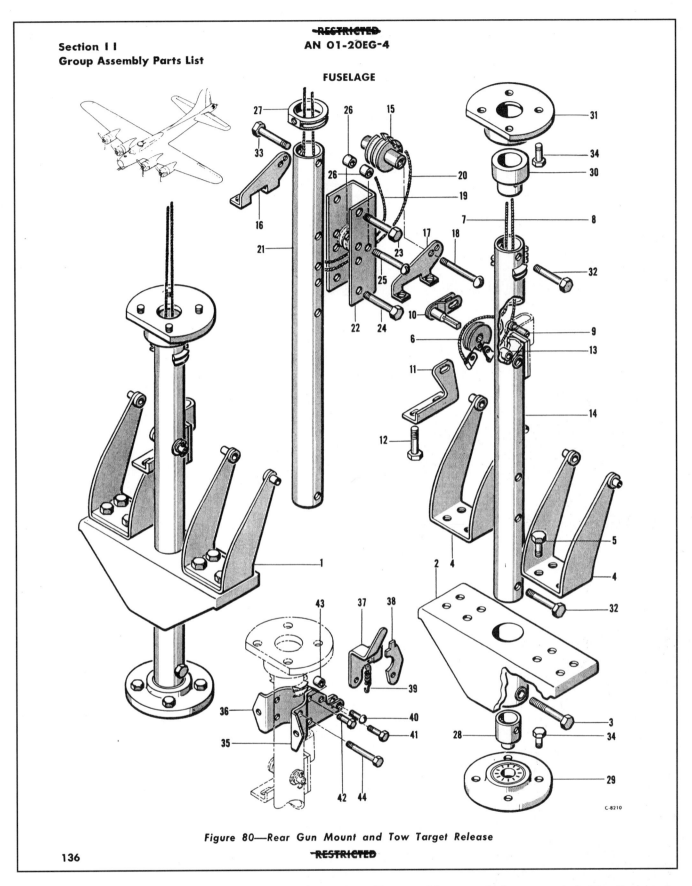

Figure 80—Rear Gun Mount and Tow Target Release

C-8210

Central column with crossbar and forks supported two .50-caliber machine guns in factory-style B-17 tail gun unit.
(Carl Scholl/Aero Trader)

AN 01-20EG-4

FUSELAGE

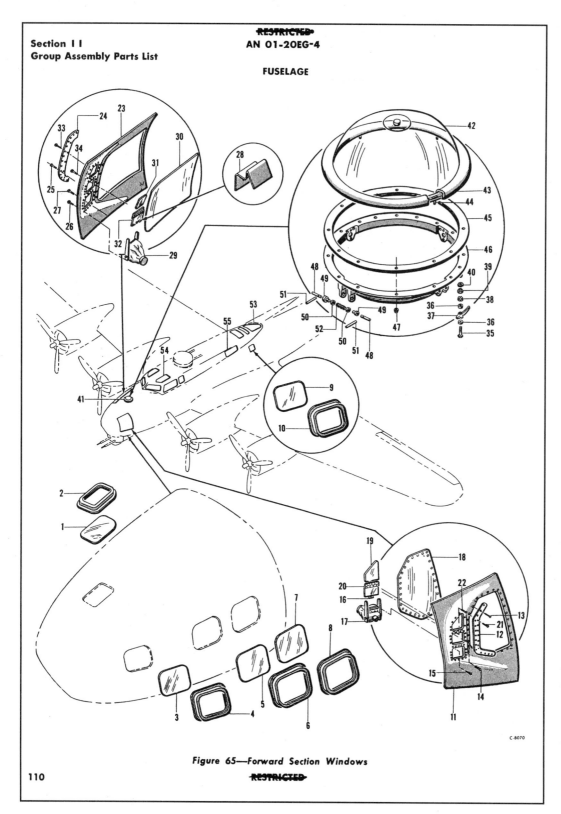

Figure 65—Forward Section Windows

110

the B-17E, and testers said it would be preferable to the Sperry upper if a good computing gunsight could be added. Without this type of sight available at the time for the Martin, the Sperry was considered superior for retention in B-17s. (Later, computing sights were available for Martin top turrets, but B-17s retained improved variations of the Sperry upper turret to the end of Fortress production.) A later comparison of the Liberator-turreted B-17E, without waist gun mounts, and a standard B-17F provided some surprises in an AAF report: "The performance of the modified B-17E as compared with the B-17F at combat conditions was approximately the same, giving a faster speed at minimum cruise power settings..., and approximately the same top speed at sea level.

The advantage of the modified B-17E was its lighter basic weight and better center of gravity location which gave the airplane better

Cheek windows on B-17Gs were heavy stampings supporting K-5 gun mounts protruding into the slipstream enough to afford more forward coverage than did previous cheek guns. Cheek gun emplacements replaced small scanning windows in the nose. Most G-models had the left cheek gun in the forward window location, with the right cheek gun in the middle window; this was the opposite placement from that used on most F-models, although a few variations occurred, especially on F-models.

FUSELAGE

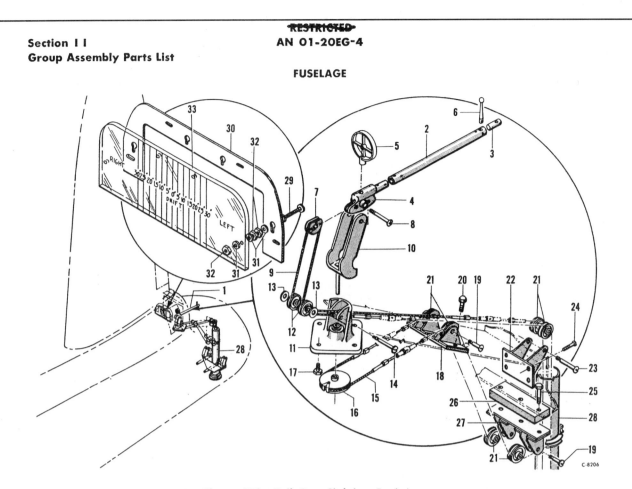

Figure 152—Tail Gun Sighting Equipment

Tail Gun Sighting Equipment

Figure & Index No.	Part Number	1 2 3 4 5 6 7 Nomenclature	Usage Code	Units Per Assy.
		Tail Gun Sighting Equipment		
	55-7377	Fuselage Assembly (see fig. 71)	All	Ref
	15-7360-83	Enclosure Assembly—Tail gun (see fig. 81)	PB	Ref
	15-7516	Installation—Rear gun sight	PB	NP
152-1	3-13519-5	Sight Assembly—Rear gun	PB	1
2	3-13519-2	Tube	PB	1
3	3-13519-1	Plug	PB	1
4	1-18296-4	Fitting—Rear gun sight	PB	1
5	1-22607	Sight Assembly—Gun ring	PB	1
6	1-18302	Bead—Rear gun sight	PB	1
7	1-26403-2	Quadrant—Rear gun sight	PB	1
8	AN3-15	Bolt—Aircraft	PB	1
9	3-13519-3	Cable Assembly	PB	1
	15-7516-1	Mount Assembly	PB	1
10	1-19087-4	Yoke Assembly—Sight mount	PB	1
11	1-18280	Support Assembly—Gun sight	PB	1
	AN201K4A	Bearing—Ball	PB	2
12	AN210-1A	Pulley—Anti-friction bearing control	PB	2
13	41-5951-40-13	Washer	PB	2
14	AN23-22	Bolt—Clevis	PB	1
15	15-7516-4	Pulley Assembly—Rear gun sight	PB	1
16	1-19083	Pulley Assembly	PB	1
17	AN3-5A	Bolt—Aircraft	PB	4
18	1-18263	Bracket Assembly—Control pulley	PB	1
19	AN23-13	Bolt—Clevis	PB	4
20	AN3-5A	Bolt—Aircraft	PB	3
21	AN210-1A	Pulley—Anti-friction bearing control	PB	6
22	1-18253	Bracket—Control pulley	PB	1
23	AN23-17	Bolt—Clevis	PB	1
24	AN520-10R8	Screw—Round head	PB	4
25	AN3-11A	Bolt—Aircraft	PB	3
26	1-18319	Spacer—Micarta	PB	1
27	1-18264	Bracket Assembly—Control pulley	PB	1
	15-7518	Installation—Rear gun mount	PB	NP
28	15-7518-1	Mount Assembly (see fig. 80)	PB	1
	15-10422	Installation—Rear gunners azimuth scale	PB	NP
29	AN526-1032-24	Screw—Truss head	PB	4
30	6-13181	Support—Azimuth scale	PB	1
31	AN960-10L	Washer—Plain	PB	16
32	AN364-1032	Nut—Self-locking	PB	12
33	6-13183	Scale—Azimuth	PB	1

Moved by cables when the guns moved, this ring-and-bead sight served in the factory tail gun emplacement on B-17s until the advent of the Cheyenne turret. (Carl Scholl/Aero Trader)

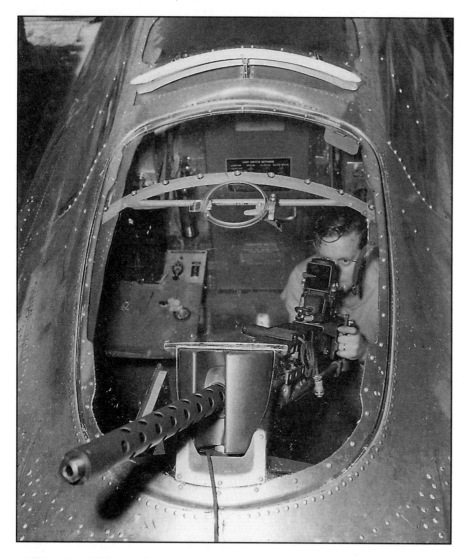

Late variation on radio room gun used K-6 gun mount in cutout in Plexiglas, allowing window to remain in place instead of being opened as on earlier Fortresses. N-8 gunsight is used. Some B-17Gs deleted the radio room gun altogether. (Boeing)

flying characteristics."[4]

Reports from combat veterans said enemy fighters sometimes waited to close for an attack until they saw the Fortress' two slab bomb bay doors open down beneath the belly of the airplane like billboards signaling the bomb run had begun. Evasive action was less likely at this time. One test proved the bomb bay doors could be kept closed until only 15 seconds before reaching the bomb release point without hampering bombing accuracy. (B-24 bomb bay doors, in contrast to Fortress doors, slid up the side of the fuselage, and provided less of a visual clue when they were open. An Eighth Air Force test not adopted for production B-17s was the use of bomb bay doors that parted and slid fore and aft along the fuselage instead of opening outward. Another Eglin test used snap-opening bomb bay doors

Looking forward in the waist of a B-17E, the photo captures cramped quarters for two gunners trying to fire simultaneously. Wind deflectors can be seen at front edges of windows. Ammunition cans gave way to flexible stainless steel chutes feeding guns from larger stationary ammunition boxes. Slipstream made traversing waist guns forward in flight more difficult than on the ground. (Peter M. Bowers collection)

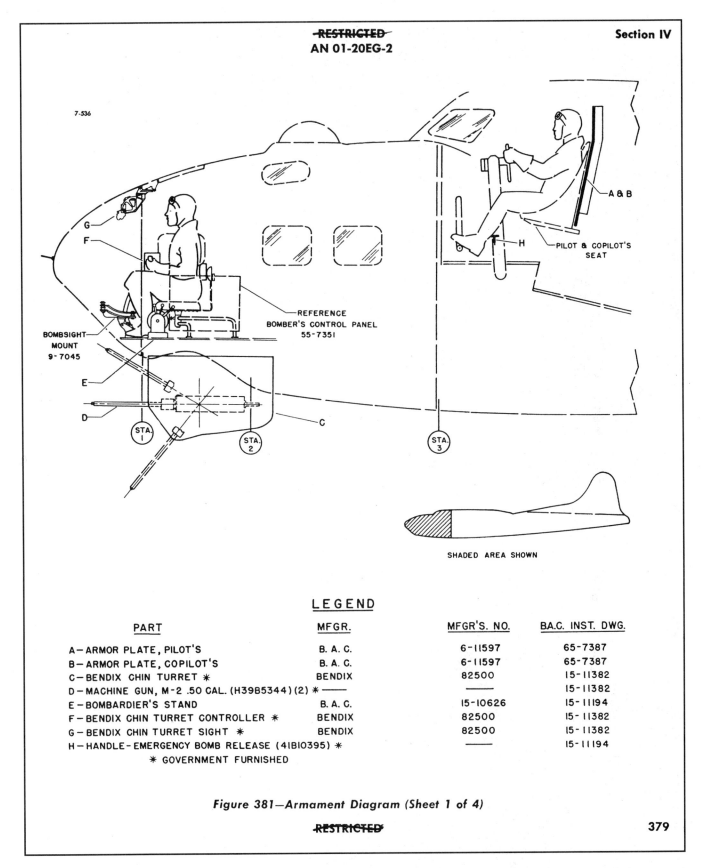

7-536

G

F

REFERENCE
BOMBER'S CONTROL PANEL
55-7351

BOMBSIGHT
MOUNT
9-7045

E

D

STA.
1

STA.
2

STA.
3

A & B

H

PILOT & COPILOT'S
SEAT

SHADED AREA SHOWN

LEGEND

PART	MFGR.	MFGR'S. NO.	B.A.C. INST. DWG.
A — ARMOR PLATE, PILOT'S	B. A. C.	6-11597	65-7387
B — ARMOR PLATE, COPILOT'S	B. A. C.	6-11597	65-7387
C — BENDIX CHIN TURRET *	BENDIX	82500	15-11382
D — MACHINE GUN, M-2 .50 CAL. (H39B5344) (2) *	——	——	15-11382
E — BOMBARDIER'S STAND	B. A. C.	15-10626	15-11194
F — BENDIX CHIN TURRET CONTROLLER *	BENDIX	82500	15-11382
G — BENDIX CHIN TURRET SIGHT *	BENDIX	82500	15-11382
H — HANDLE — EMERGENCY BOMB RELEASE (41B10395) *	——	——	15-11194

* GOVERNMENT FURNISHED

Figure 381—Armament Diagram (Sheet 1 of 4)

Sitting atop the Bendix A-16 chin turret, the bombardier in a B-17G had a head-on view of oncoming fighters, and of his target on the ground far below. Gunsight for chin turret mounted in overhead bracket (part G), as depicted in the B-17G erection and maintenance manual. (Carl Scholl/Aero Trader)

Boeing workers installed a K-6 enclosed waist gun mount on a B-17G. Plate inside fuselage beneath gun is armor protection. Bell E-11 recoil adaptor and ring sight are used. (Boeing)

that could be activated only 10 seconds from bombs-away; it did not see production.)

When AAF tests of B-17Fs began late in 1942, one of the first was a pioneering chin turret installation in aircraft 41-24341, later evolved into the B-40 escort version armament, and on to the B-17G. In fact, although the chin turret is generally used as the chief recognition feature of the B-17G, it was first envisioned as an addition to existing F-model production. A later B-17F

B-17G K-6 waist gun installation photo from January 1945 shows flexible ammo feed chute leading from wooden box mounted on side of fuselage. This installation is fitted with N-8 electric gunsight; late-war K-7 gun mounts, similar in appearance to K-6, used gears and cables to feed azimuth and elevation information to compensating K-13 gunsight. (Boeing)

WARBIRDTECH
SERIES

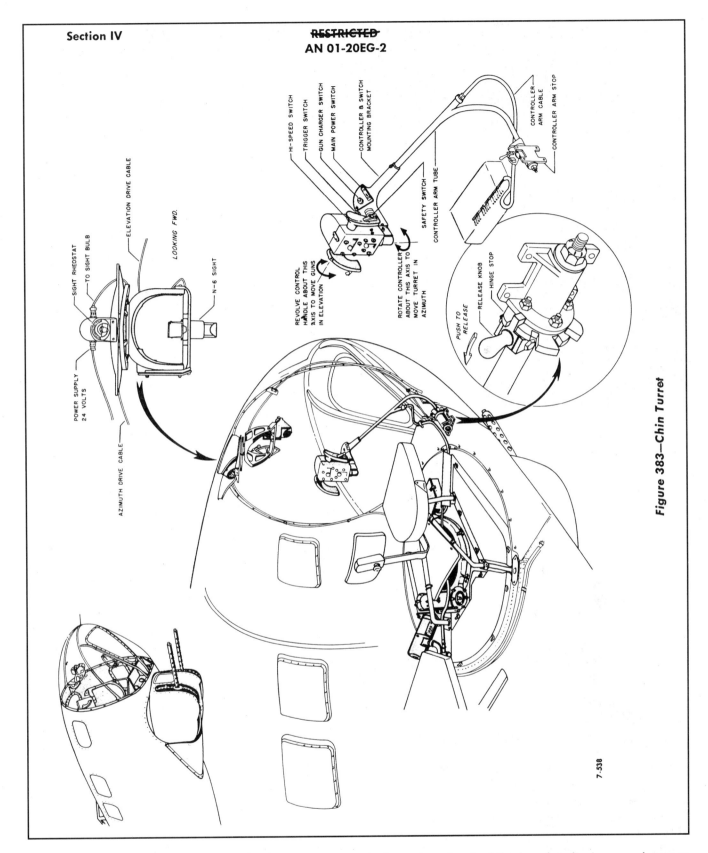

Figure 383—Chin Turret

HI-SPEED SWITCH
TRIGGER SWITCH
GUN CHARGER SWITCH
MAIN POWER SWITCH
CONTROLLER & SWITCH MOUNTING BRACKET
CONTROLLER ARM TUBE
SAFETY SWITCH
CONTROLLER ARM CABLE
CONTROLLER ARM STOP

REVOLVE CONTROL HANDLE ABOUT THIS AXIS TO MOVE GUNS IN ELEVATION

ROTATE CONTROLLER ABOUT THIS AXIS TO MOVE TURRET IN AZIMUTH

PUSH TO RELEASE
RELEASE KNOB
HINGE STOP

SIGHT RHEOSTAT
TO SIGHT BULB
ELEVATION DRIVE CABLE
LOOKING FWD.
N-6 SIGHT
POWER SUPPLY 24 VOLTS
AZIMUTH DRIVE CABLE

7-538

Bendix chin turret operating control grip was on an arm that stowed out of the bombardier's way when not needed. Grips were elevated or depressed to move guns vertically; the controller unit was pivoted left or right to traverse the guns. Cables for azimuth and elevation drive were routed to the overhead gunsight bracket to align it with the movement of the turret. (Carl Scholl/Aero Trader)

armament suitability test used aircraft 42-30631 which also sported a chin turret. Staggered waist windows (under consideration since late 1942 as a way to give gunners more elbow room) were introduced on this test F-model, and after experimenting with Boeing and K-5 waist gun mounts, large can-shaped K-6 mounts were installed, making 42-30631 an archetype for the B-17G series in many respects. A test report filed in January 1944 chronicled the use of an enclosed radio compartment gun in a B-17F. Using a K-6 gun mount in a cutout in the radio compartment's Plexiglas hatch, this installation afforded the radio operator enclosed comfort.[5] (Enclosed K-6 radio room gun mounts appeared on portions of B-17G production. A local Eighth Air Force modification to some B-17s used a heavy aluminum plate into which a K-5 mount was fitted, the whole unit replacing the aft end of the radio hatch.)

Early version of Bendix chin turret was the best new feature of the B-40 escort variant of the Flying Fortress. B-40 also used an extra dorsal turret (a Martin) in the radio room location, with an abbreviated decking ahead of it. (USAF)

A proposal not adopted was the creation of a prone station for the bombardier in B-17F number 42-29729 in late 1943. And from 1 December 1943 to 15 February 1944, three B-17Fs were scheduled for cold weather tests at Ladd Field, Fairbanks, Alaska, to determine whether B-17s were suitable for operations at extremely low temperatures. When one of the Fortresses crashed before the start of the tests, it was replaced by a B-17G. Even though aircraft

Original feed setup for twin waist guns of YB-40 needed alterations after combat trial over Europe. (USAF)

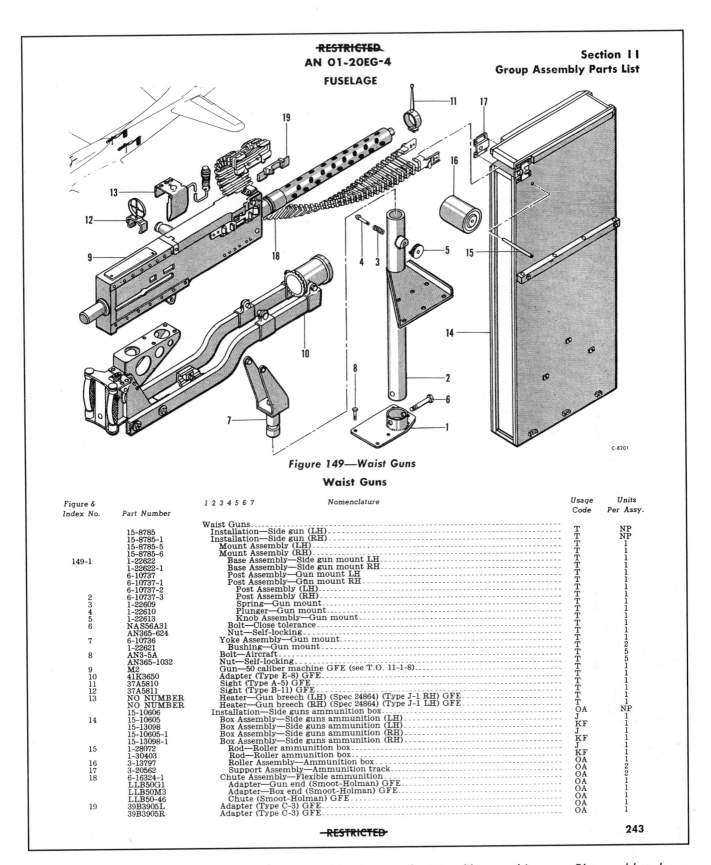

C-8201

Figure 149—Waist Guns

Waist Guns

Figure & Index No.	Part Number	1 2 3 4 5 6 7 Nomenclature	Usage Code	Units Per Assy.
		Waist Guns		
	15-8785	Installation—Side gun (LH)	T	NP
	15-8785-1	Installation—Side gun (RH)	T	NP
	15-8785-5	Mount Assembly (LH)	T	1
	15-8785-6	Mount Assembly (RH)	T	1
149-1	1-22622	Base Assembly—Side gun mount LH	T	1
	1-22622-1	Base Assembly—Side gun mount RH	T	1
	6-10737	Post Assembly—Gun mount LH	T	1
	6-10737-1	Post Assembly—Gun mount RH	T	1
	6-10737-2	Post Assembly (LH)	T	1
2	6-10737-3	Post Assembly (RH)	T	1
3	1-22609	Spring—Gun mount	T	1
4	1-22610	Plunger—Gun mount	T	1
5	1-22613	Knob Assembly—Gun mount	T	1
6	NAS56A31	Bolt—Close tolerance	T	1
	AN365-624	Nut—Self-locking	T	1
7	6-10736	Yoke Assembly—Gun mount	T	2
	1-22621	Bushing—Gun mount	T	5
8	AN3-5A	Bolt—Aircraft	T	5
	AN365-1032	Nut—Self-locking	T	5
9	M2	Gun—50 caliber machine GFE (see T.O. 11-1-8)	T	1
10	41K3650	Adapter (Type E-8) GFE	T	1
11	37A5810	Sight (Type A-5) GFE	T	1
12	37A5811	Sight (Type B-11) GFE	T	1
13	NO NUMBER	Heater—Gun breech (LH) (Spec 24864) (Type J-1 RH) GFE	T	1
	NO NUMBER	Heater—Gun breech (RH) (Spec 24864) (Type J-1 LH) GFE	OA	NP
14	15-10606	Installation—Side guns ammunition box	J	1
	15-10605	Box Assembly—Side guns ammunition (LH)	KF	1
	15-13098	Box Assembly—Side guns ammunition (LH)	KF	1
	15-10605-1	Box Assembly—Side guns ammunition (RH)	KF	1
	15-13098-1	Box Assembly—Side guns ammunition (RH)	J	1
15	1-28072	Rod—Roller ammunition box	KF	2
	1-30403	Rod—Roller ammunition box	OA	2
16	3-13797	Roller Assembly—Ammunition box	OA	2
17	3-20562	Support Assembly—Ammunition track	OA	1
18	6-16324-1	Chute Assembly—Flexible ammunition	OA	1
	LLB50G1	Adapter—Gun end (Smoot-Holman) GFE	OA	1
	LLB50M3	Adapter—Box end (Smoot-Holman) GFE	OA	1
	LLB50-46	Chute (Smoot-Holman) GFE	OA	1
19	39B3905L	Adapter (Type C-3) GFE	OA	1
	39B3905R	Adapter (Type C-3) GFE	OA	1

Open-style waist windows on B-17s often used E-8 recoil mount for .50-caliber machine gun. Ring-and-bead gun sight depicted in drawing includes type B-11 ring sight mounted on gun receiver and type A-5 bead sight on muzzle end of barrel cooling jacket. Tall ammunition box (part 14) fed the gun through flexible chute, as seen in a B-17G Dash-4 illustrated parts book. (Carl Scholl/Aero Trader)

NEW FEED

Revised feed for YB-40 used larger ammo cans placed farther from guns than original version. Ultimately, performance of heavy YB-40 doomed its future, especially since it did not contribute bombs on target.

operating anywhere in the world encountered sub-zero temperatures at bombing altitude, they typically returned to warmer temperatures within hours as they returned to base. The purpose of the Alaska tests was to cold-soak the aircraft, to see if they retained operational suitability in prolonged cold temperatures. The tested B-17s of 1943-44 were ultimately considered "operationally unsatisfactory for temperatures below minus 30 degrees Fahrenheit because of the small percentage of airplanes which can be maintained in commission. This is due to increased malfunctions, winterization equipment not installed, and unsatisfactory winterization items." However, this still was an improvement over previous

YB-40 side view shows revised tail gun window configuration applied to the B-40. Ball turret appears to be experimental partially retractable version.

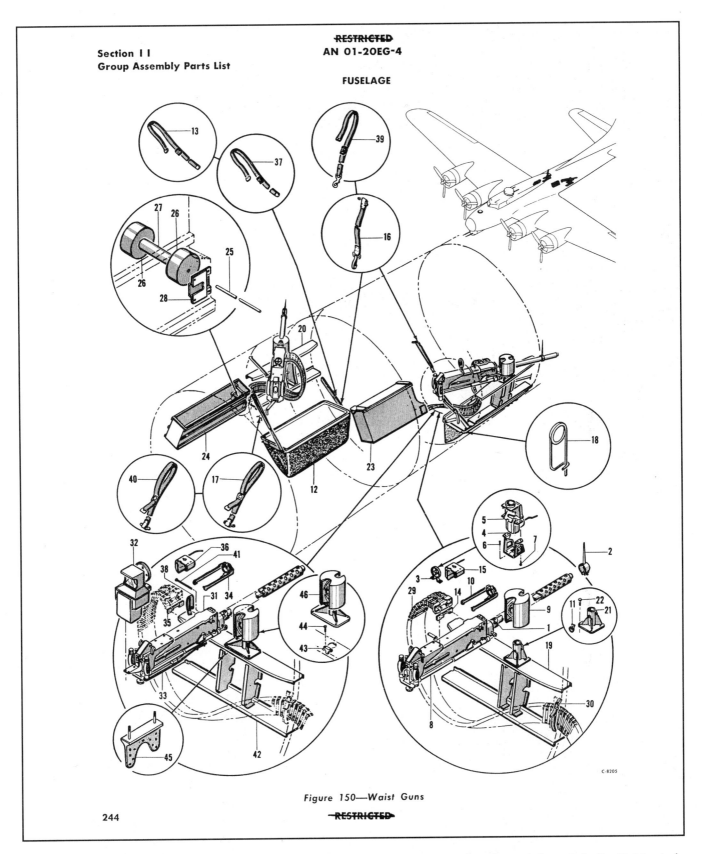

Figure 150—Waist Guns

C-8205

Drawing from B-17G parts manual shows wide-footed K-7 gun mount in circle at lower left, and similar K-6 in circle at right. K-7 mount was intended for use with E-13 recoil adaptor which had provision for mounting large K-13 compensating gunsight. Azimuth and elevation information for the gunsight was cabled from the mount. Shell-catching hoppers beneath guns made the floor safer to walk during a running fight. (Carl Scholl/Aero Trader)

In a test, about 60 equipped combat soldiers could fit in a B-17 for transport to a forward airfield.

winter tests of B-17s, and Fortresses were preferred over Liberators for cold weather operation: "The B-17 is the most satisfactory type heavy bombardment airplane for low temperature operations," AAF testers said.[6]

B-17Gs returned to Ladd Field in the winter of 1944-45 for more cold-weather testing. An AAF historical summary said: "Although the B-17G could be operated at ground temperatures as low as minus 49 degrees Fahrenheit, it was not con-

sidered suitable for extreme low-temperature operation because of engine difficulties, erratic propeller feathering, an unsatisfactory manual fuel primer, and an unsatisfactory cabin heating system." Armament operated well, although less cum-

Some B-17Gs were modified to carry a pair of U.S.-copied buzz bombs for tests at Eglin, Florida, and Wendover, Utah. Weight of the buzz bombs was ponderous. (USAF)

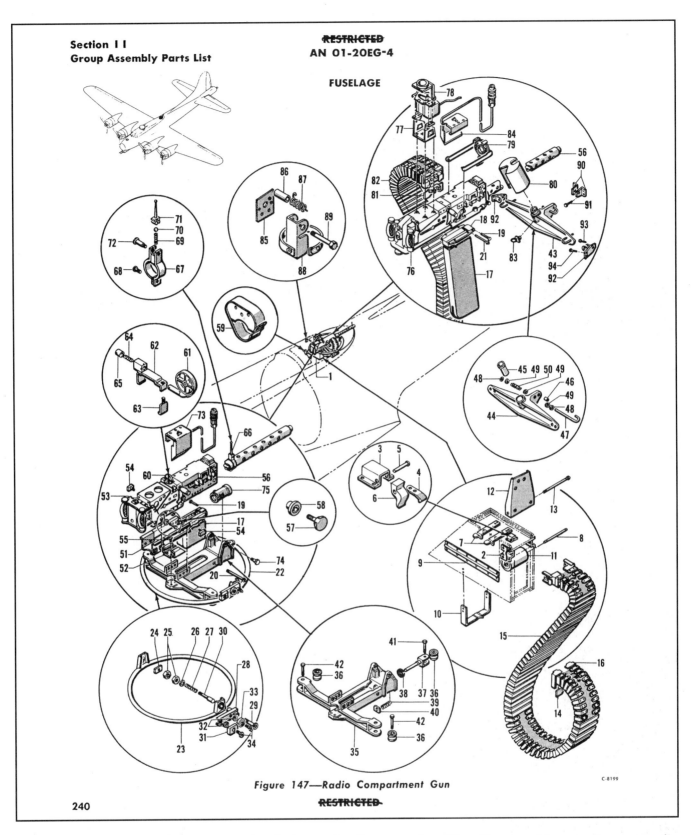

FUSELAGE

Figure 147—Radio Compartment Gun

C-8199

Drawing from B-17G illustrated parts book shows ring for mounting .50-caliber machine gun in open radio compartment window (drawn in large circle to the left), and later enclosed variation using a K-6 mount (see circle at upper right of drawing). Ring sight for open-air version folds down for stowage (parts 61-65). Experience showed ammunition would feed more smoothly to the radio room gun if the flexible chute's open side was reversed part way down its length, as seen in part 15.

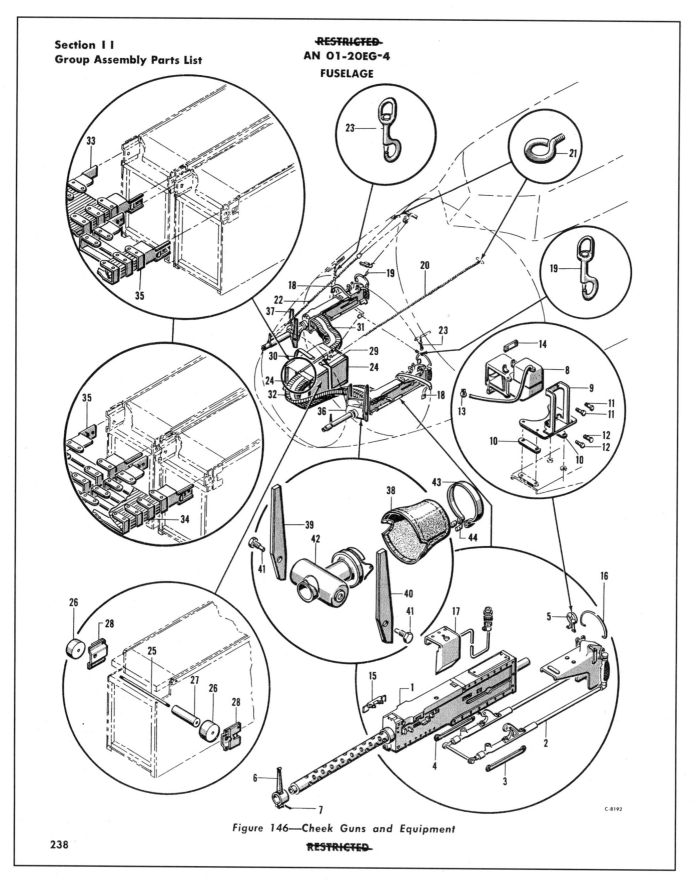

Figure 146—Cheek Guns and Equipment

C-8192

*Details of B-17G cheek gun mounts include stylized picture of K-5 mount (part 42) and E-11 recoil adaptor (part 2).
(Carl Scholl/Aero Trader)*

bersome arctic clothing was urged for gunners in the Sperry turrets.[7]

When B-17Gs came under test scrutiny, the Cheyenne tail turret received positive reviews. Tested in B-17G number 42-31435 and reported in January 1944, the Cheyenne installation was named for the Cheyenne, Wyoming, B-17 modification center. Previous tests with boosted Bell tail gun emplacements still were first choice of the Eglin testers, but in reality, the Cheyenne mount was put into production on G-models, as well as being retrofitted to earlier B-17Gs in the field. Testers said the Cheyenne installation "is approximately four times as accurate as the standard B-17 tail guns. However, the Bell power mount in a B-17 tail proved twelve to fifteen times as accurate as the standard installation..."[8] The Cheyenne mount still used a central

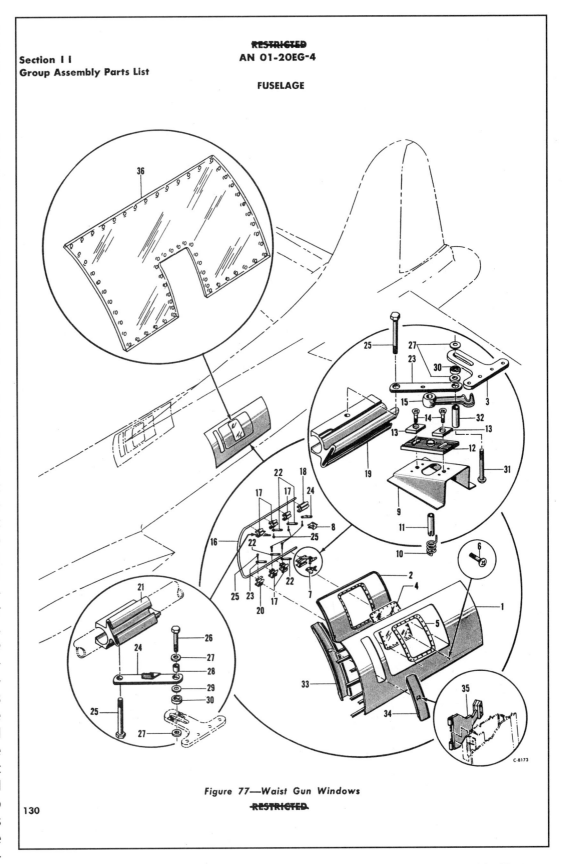

Figure 77—Waist Gun Windows

RESTRICTED

130

B-17G waist gun drawing shows early style opening window (part 2) with wind baffle (part 34). Later one-piece Plexiglas closed window with cutout for K-6 or (with modifications) K-7 mount is depicted as part number 36.

~~RESTRICTED~~
AN 01-2OEG-4

FUSELAGE

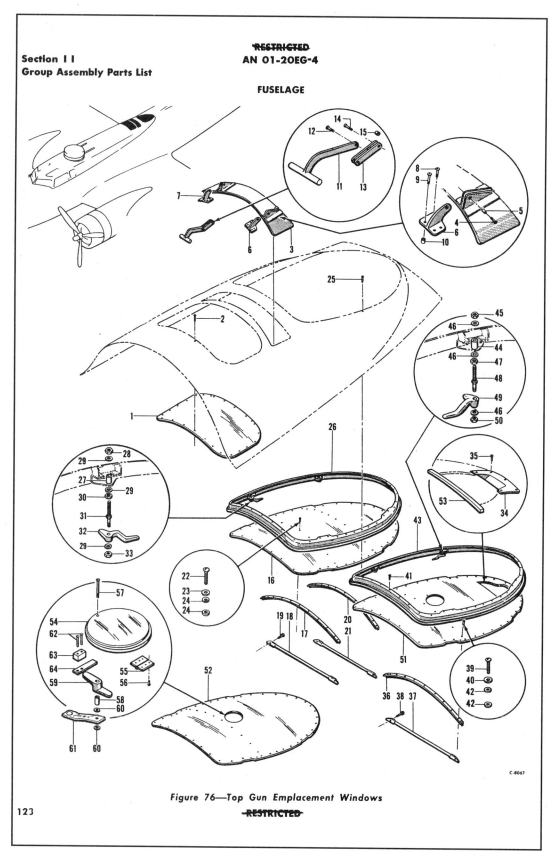

Figure 76—Top Gun Emplacement Windows

~~RESTRICTED~~

123

column supporting two narrowly-spaced side-by-side .50-caliber guns in E-11 recoil adapters. A rounded aluminum shroud provided greater movement for the guns, while an enlarged curved Plexiglas window increased visibility. A flat plate of armor glass inside the emplacement protected the gunner.

As reported in February 1944, the AAF Proving Ground Command investigated the possibility of using the B-17G's A-16 chin turret while simultaneously operating the M-9 Norden bombsight. The chin turret used grips and triggers on a swing-out arm normally stowed at the side of the fuselage; its gunsight was suspended from the ceiling. The testers' verdict said: "The turret operated very well when used separately from the bomb sight, but large bombing errors occurred when the turret and M-9 bomb sight were used simultane-

Varieties of B-17G radio room hatches include part 51, with cutout for K-6 mount. Part 3 is extendable wind deflector in front of hatch, as shown in illustrated parts book. (Carl Scholl/Aero Trader)

88

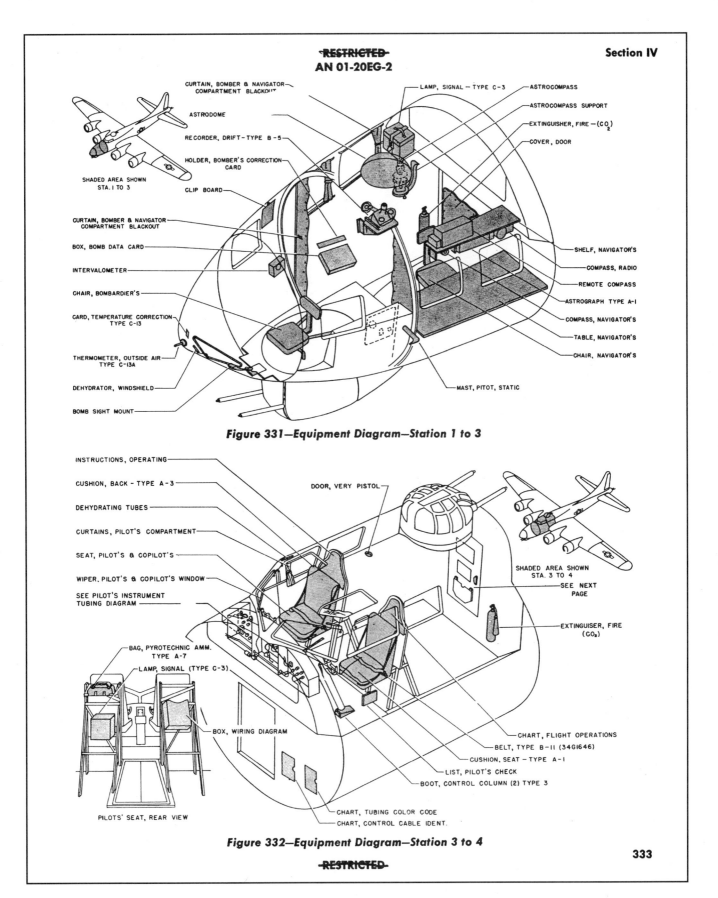

Figure 331—Equipment Diagram—Station 1 to 3

Figure 332—Equipment Diagram—Station 3 to 4

333

Detailed equipment drawings from the Dash-2 erection and maintenance manual show locations of furnishings in nose and cockpit of a B-17G. (Carl Scholl/Aero Trader)

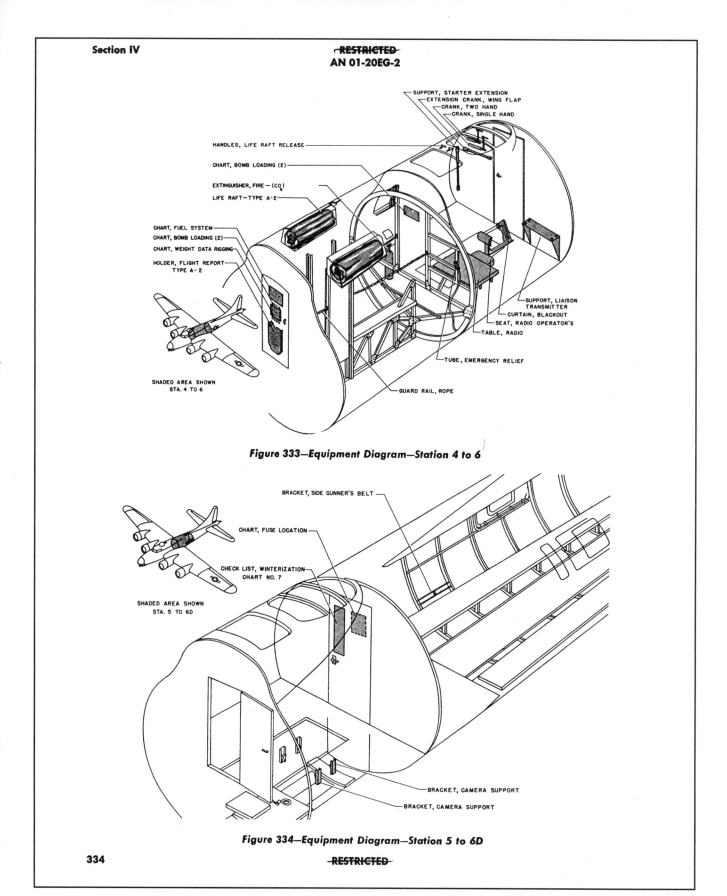

SUPPORT, STARTER EXTENSION
EXTENSION CRANK, WING FLAP
CRANK, TWO HAND
CRANK, SINGLE HAND

HANDLES, LIFE RAFT RELEASE

CHART, BOMB LOADING (2)

EXTINGUISHER, FIRE — (CO_2)
LIFE RAFT—TYPE A-2

CHART, FUEL SYSTEM
CHART, BOMB LOADING (2)
CHART, WEIGHT DATA RIGGING
HOLDER, FLIGHT REPORT
TYPE A-2

SUPPORT, LIAISON
TRANSMITTER
CURTAIN, BLACKOUT
SEAT, RADIO OPERATOR'S
TABLE, RADIO

TUBE, EMERGENCY RELIEF

SHADED AREA SHOWN
STA. 4 TO 6

GUARD RAIL, ROPE

Figure 333—Equipment Diagram—Station 4 to 6

BRACKET, SIDE GUNNER'S BELT

CHART, FUSE LOCATION

CHECK LIST, WINTERIZATION
CHART NO. 7

SHADED AREA SHOWN
STA. 5 TO 6D

BRACKET, CAMERA SUPPORT
BRACKET, CAMERA SUPPORT

Figure 334—Equipment Diagram—Station 5 to 6D

~~RESTRICTED~~

Bomb bay and radio room drawings from B-17G erection and maintenance manual show placement of detail accessories. (Carl Scholl/Aero Trader)

WARBIRDTECH
S E R I E S

ously. All bombardiers and gunners who participated in the test agreed that it was not possible to track another airplane and to bomb at the same time. When the N-6 gunsight was lowered from the ceiling there was not sufficient room for the bombardier to look through the optics of the M-9 bomb sight. It was recommended that simultaneous operation of the M-9 bomb sight and A-16 turret in the B-17G not be attempted."[9]

The tests described here are only a fraction of the evaluations given the Flying Fortress by the USAAF and Boeing. The acceleration of technological advances during World War Two mandated continuous evaluations of tools like the B-17.

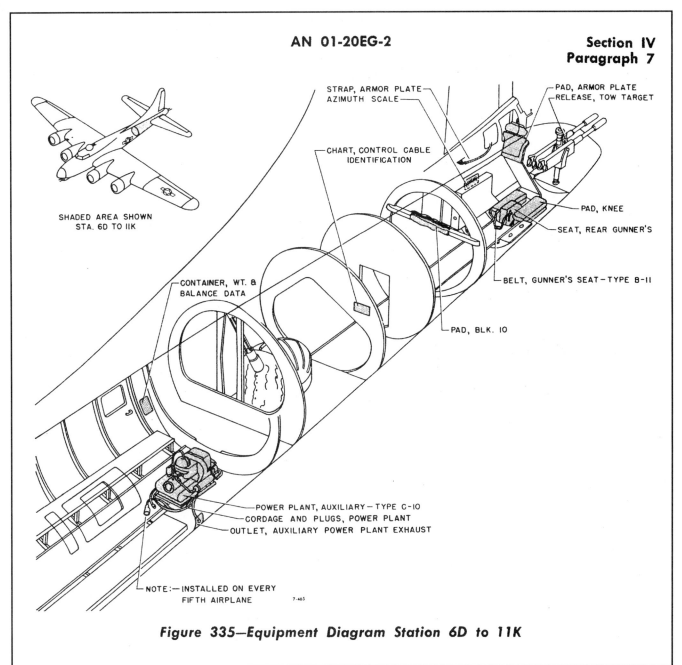

AN 01-20EG-2

Section IV
Paragraph 7

SHADED AREA SHOWN STA. 6D TO IIK

STRAP, ARMOR PLATE AZIMUTH SCALE

PAD, ARMOR PLATE RELEASE, TOW TARGET

CHART, CONTROL CABLE IDENTIFICATION

PAD, KNEE

SEAT, REAR GUNNER'S

BELT, GUNNER'S SEAT—TYPE B-II

CONTAINER, WT. & BALANCE DATA

PAD, BLK. IO

POWER PLANT, AUXILIARY — TYPE C-IO
CORDAGE AND PLUGS, POWER PLANT
OUTLET, AUXILIARY POWER PLANT EXHAUST

NOTE:— INSTALLED ON EVERY FIFTH AIRPLANE

7-465

Figure 335—Equipment Diagram Station 6D to 11K

Provisions for the tail gunner included a protective pad on fuselage structure forward of his station. Some B-17s were equipped with a Type C-10 auxiliary power plant in the aft waist section. (Carl Scholl/Aero Trader)

1 "History of the Army Air Forces Proving Ground Command — Part Twelve: Testing of the B-17 and B-24," by Historical Branch, AAF Proving Ground Command, Eglin Field, Florida, July 1945. 2 *Ibid.* 3 *Ibid.* 4 *Ibid.* 5 *Ibid.* 6 *Ibid.* 7 *Ibid.* 8 *Ibid.* 9 *Ibid.*

POSTWAR 5 FORTRESSES

AN OLD, BUT EXPENDABLE, FRIEND

The largesse of American victory in 1945 soon melted into a stoic Cold War determination that enfolded the B-17 in its convolutions. The U.S. Army Air Forces, soon to become the separate U.S. Air Force, had more B-17s on hand in 1945 than it could use. In this atmosphere of plenty, B-17s were scrapped with but few tears shed. But the Fortress survived in the postwar Air Force in greater numbers than did the Liberator. With an entire arsenal to pick from, B-17s came to the fore as VIP transports as the Air Force quickly dismembered its B-24 fleet, and kept B-29s around in bombing

SB-17G 44-83722 posed for a portrait with a rescue L-5 during a transition period in markings; fuselage star of B-17 has red stripe mandated in 1948, but insignia on wing does not carry the red stripe yet. Wing/fuselage center section outlined in black was painted yellow with rescue lettering and numbering in black. This Fortress served in Dhahran after the war, and could be outfitted with the air-droppable lifeboat. After a variety of assignments, 44-83722 was flown to Yucca Flats, Nevada, in 1952 for use on the ground to show the effects of nuclear blasts. (See also color section in this volume for a photo of this aircraft taken after one of the nuclear tests.) Portions of this SB-17, including the forward fuselage, were saved and may be rebuilt as part of a Fortress restoration.

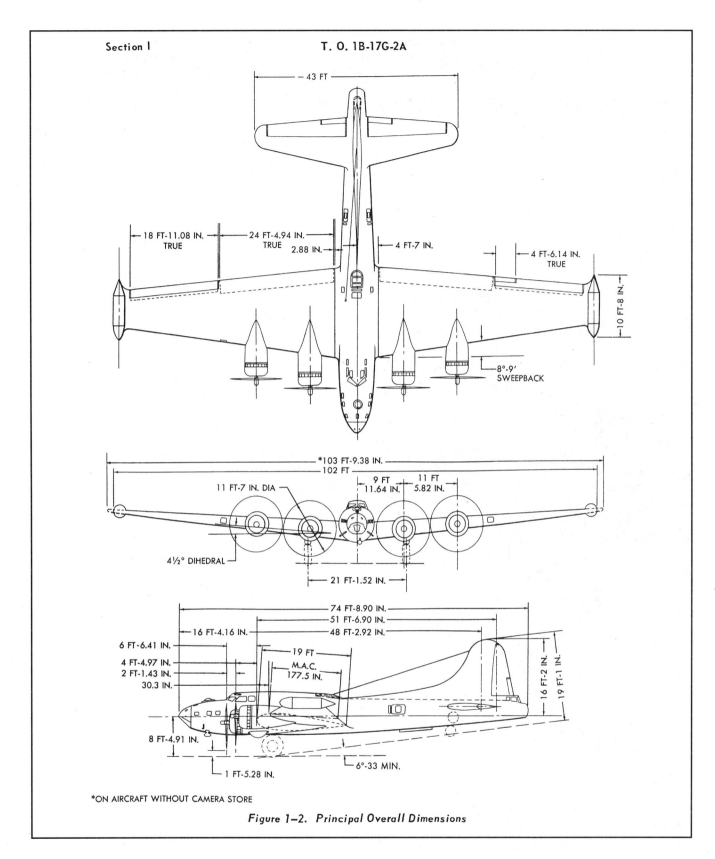

Figure 1–2. Principal Overall Dimensions

*ON AIRCRAFT WITHOUT CAMERA STORE

Revamped three-view drawing taken from a drone supplement to the B-17 erection and maintenance manual shows wingspan configuration and dimensions with and without tip pods for cameras. Updated from existing artwork, this drawing inaccurately shows old style waist windows instead of staggered enclosures common to the B-17Gs converted to drone operations after the war. (Keller/Sturges/Columbia Airmotive)

hazardous skies by manned DB-17 director aircraft. Still other surviving Air Force Flying Fortresses were parked in the Nevada desert varying distances from ground zero. Nuclear blasts twisted and puffed at least one airframe, and sprinkled another B-17G with enough radioactivity to keep it off limits until the mid-1960s.

SB-17G 44-83700, bearing buzz number BA-700 on vertical fin, releases its lifeboat. (USAF)

roles. Stripped of armaments and armor plate, lightened B-17Gs were eminently serviceable as transports. While the U.S. Navy used its investment in Privateers until 1964 (as drones) and even kept a few PB4Y-1P Liberators in photo squadron service into the 1950s, the last B-24 to wear an Air Force star was a late Ford B-24M on a bailment contract in 1954.

To the Air Force, the B-17 still had a touch of art deco glamour,

although sentimentality was not a hallmark of that newest branch of the military in the post-World War Two years. When planners envisioned anti-aircraft missiles to defend America against Soviet bomber strikes, the Air Force readily adapted some of its Flying Fortresses as QB-17 drones to play target for the missiles. To sample radioactivity during 1946 atmospheric nuclear tests at Bikini atoll in the South Pacific, yellow-and-silver QB-17s were shepherded into

Search-and-rescue units kept SB-17s in service after the war. Stateside detachments at locations including Hamilton Field, California, and McChord Field, Washington, complemented overseas postings like the Third Air Rescue Squadron at Johnson Air Base, Japan.

On 25 June 1950, in what has been described as the first Air Rescue Service mission of the Korean War, 1 Lt. James A. Scheib was aircraft commander aboard armed SB-17G number 44-83885, tasked to carry Col. William H.S. Wright, chief of

Disassembled and moved from a town park to the local airport at Stuttgart, Arkansas, circa 1953, B-17F 42-29782 was reassembled and used for many years as a sprayer and air tanker, carrying civil registration N17W. In 1985, Seattle businessman and flier Bob Richardson bought N17W to make it available for the Museum of Flight in Washington state. Volunteers using space at Boeing rebuilt N17W to wartime configuration. (Max Biegert collection)

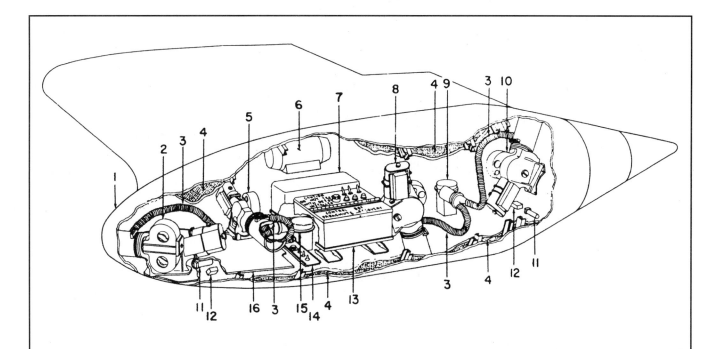

1 LEFT-HAND CAMERA STORE	6 DYNAMOTOR	12 CONDENSER
2 NO. 1 CAMERA	7 TIME-CODE GENERATOR	13 PARACHUTE RECOVERY CONTROL BOX
3 HEATER DUCT	8 NO. 3 CAMERA	14 SWITCH PANEL
4 INSULATION	9 AFT HEATER	15 FORWARD HEATER
5 NO. 2 CAMERA	10 NO. 4 CAMERA	16 FLOOR
	11 THERMOSWITCH	

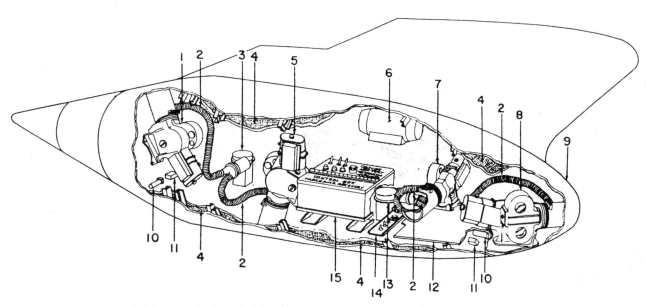

1 NO. 4 CAMERA	6 DYNAMOTOR	11 CONDENSER
2 HEATER DUCT	7 NO. 2 CAMERA	12 FLOOR
3 AFT HEATER	8 NO. 1 CAMERA	13 FORWARD HEATER
4 INSULATION	9 RIGHT HAND CAMERA STORE	14 SWITCH PANEL
5 NO. 3 CAMERA	10 THERMOSWITCH	15 PARACHUTE RECOVERY CONTROL BOX

Cutaway views show cameras and hardware inside QB-17 tip pods. (Keller/Sturges/Columbia Airmotive)

Hybridized for use by Curtiss-Wright as a testbed after World War Two, B-17G 44-85813 had its cockpit mounted farther aft to accommodate a central nacelle which sometimes carried a turboprop engine, as depicted here, and sometimes mounted variations on the R-3350 reciprocating powerplant. Following its service with Curtiss-Wright, this Fortress was acquired by air tanker operator Arnold Kolb. Starting in 1969, Kolb grafted a standard B-17G nose back onto the abbreviated airframe and returned this B-17 to flight status as a more or less standard B-17G fire bomber. Registered N6694C, this B-17 was substantially damaged in a mishap at Bear Pen Airport in North Carolina in 1980. Its remains were acquired by restorer Tom Reilly, who moved parts of it to Florida pending their use in a restoration. (USAF)

The Curtiss-Wright testbed mounted a reciprocating R-3350 engine in the center location when photographed on 17 May 1958. Paddle-bladed Curtiss Electric propellers, a rarity for Fortress use, were fitted to the four Wright Cyclone engines on this aircraft. (USAF)

the Korean Military Assistance Advisory Group, from Japan back to Korea in the midst of opening hostilities instigated by North Korea. Scheib recalled his crew was on alert that day, and received a tasking "directing us to prepare a fully-armed SB-17 to transport high ranking officials from Haneda Airport, Tokyo, to Kimpo Airport, Seoul, Korea. The SB-17 assigned to us that day had an A-1 lifeboat mounted

A QB-17G drone with recording camera wingtip pods was photographed in the 1950s. Last QB-17 was downed by another Boeing product, a Bomarc missile, in 1960. (Gordon S. Williams collection)

WARBIRD**TECH**
SERIES

B-17G 44-38635 was an air tanker registered N3702G operated by TBM, Incorporated, out of Chino, California, when photographed by the author in September 1969. A true Boeing-built survivor, 44-38635 eventually ended fire service to become a static display at the Castle Air Museum on the site of the now-closed Castle Air Force Base in Atwater, California.

on its belly. The un-needed lifeboat was removed by armament personnel who also loaded the caliber .50 machine guns."[1]

Lieutenant Scheib's instrument-flight sortie into Korea required improvisation: "Before our planned instrument let-down and low approach to the Kimpo Airport (four hours of our six-hour, 40-minute flight was in weather), our radio operator received a message on his liaison radio from Headquarters Far Eastern Air Forces directing me to not land at Kimpo, but to proceed to Pusan, Korea." Later, Scheib learned Kimpo was under attack by North Korean Yak-15 fighters, and it was prudent to keep the lone Flying Fortress away. Scheib described the Pusan airfield at that time as abandoned, with no instrument approach equipment. "...We had only a World War Two regional map that showed gross topographical information and minimal data concerning the airfield at Pusan," he recalled. En route, Scheib radioed Fukuoka Control on a VHF frequency, requesting information about Pusan Airfield to help him land at the field. "They replied that they had none, but would check further. Approximately 15 minutes later, they called and said they had located a pilot in the officers' club who had '...landed a C-47 at Pusan a couple of years ago, and the strip wasn't too bad.' With that information, I told Fukuoka Control that I would attempt a landing at Pusan," Scheib related.[2]

With cloud cover extending from the Korean peninsula over the Sea of Japan, Scheib's crew coordinated a radar let-down over water to preclude flying into high terrain. "We

Unique among Flying Fortresses was B-17F air tanker N1340N, converted in 1970 by the mounting of Rolls Royce Dart turboprop engines from a Viscount airliner. To preserve center of gravity and accommodate the long turbine engines, the propellers extended nearly to the nose of the B-17. N1340N crashed in October 1970 while fighting fires. It was photographed at Wenatchee, Washington, while responding to fires in north central Washington state in July 1970. (Frederick A. Johnsen)

The author inspected turboprop Fortress N1340N at Wenatchee, Washington during its brief tenure as a propjet fire bomber. Its crew sometimes operated this Fortress on only two of its four Dart engines after it dropped its retardant, so powerful were the Rolls Royce turboprop installations. N1340N had previously operated as a conventionally-powered fire bomber, after being rescued from oblivion at the Clarkston, Washington, airport in the early 1950s by Bob Sturges. Its military serial was 42-6107. (Kenneth G. Johnsen)

broke out at about 400 feet above the sea and headed west. Standing between the seats and using his map, my navigator tried to identify coastal landmarks and he gave me headings," Scheib said. "I chose an airspeed that gave me a minimum forward speed with a little extra for an emergency. On our first probing attempt, we flew between two hills and penetrated perhaps a mile when I determined that I could not see far enough ahead to assure room for a climb-out. With engine controls pre-set for climb conditions, I advanced the throttles and was immediately enveloped in instrument conditions." Scheib and crew put the SB-17 in a spiral climb and made a second radar let-down back over the flat sea. "This time we barely penetrated the coast at 300 feet when we were suddenly on instruments. We again climbed out and I realized that even if we could locate the field at Pusan I would be unable to maneuver at 300 feet to line up for final approach on an abandoned airfield at which the landing surface condition was unknown to me. When we reached an altitude at which I could contact Fukuoka Control, I informed them of the odds of successfully completing my mission and I was subsequently directed to proceed to Itazuki Air Base, Japan, where we landed at 2035 hours." The weather improved at Kimpo that night, and another aircraft ultimately slipped in under cover of darkness with Colonel Wright, returning him to Korea.[3]

It was clearly not in the best interests of a lone SB-17 to face North Korean fighters, but photos indicate Air Force search-and-rescue Fortresses sometimes were armed during the Korean War just in case.

CIVILIAN CAREERS

The release of surplus Air Force, Navy, and Coast Guard Fortresses in the 1950s and into the early 1960s gave civilian fire bomber operators a large aircraft capable of tanking

A landmark in Milwaukie, Oregon, for decades after World War Two is this B-17G, mounted over gas pumps on old Highway 99. When photographed in early 1976, the gas station still served motorists; it has since stopped pumping gasoline, although the property is still maintained. As of this writing, efforts are being made to restore the B-17, and reverse years of exposure to wet Oregon weather. (Frederick A. Johnsen)

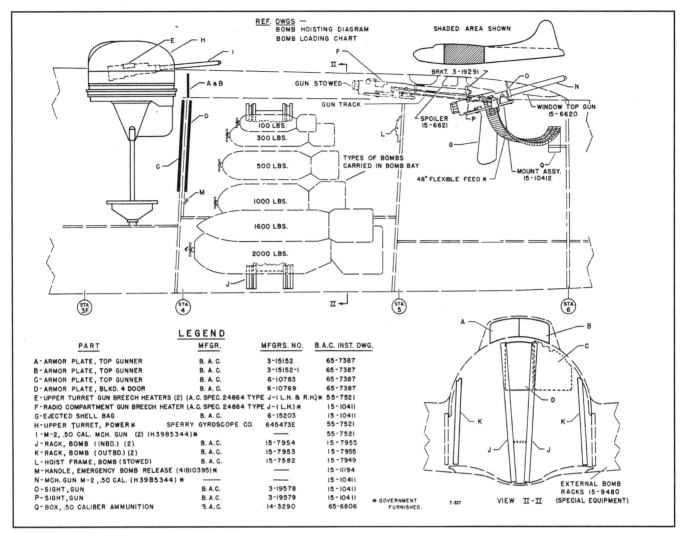

REF. DWGS —
BOMB HOISTING DIAGRAM
BOMB LOADING CHART

SHADED AREA SHOWN

BRKT. 3-19291

GUN STOWED

GUN TRACK

100 LBS.

300 LBS.

500 LBS.

1000 LBS.

1600 LBS.

2000 LBS.

TYPES OF BOMBS
CARRIED IN BOMB BAY

SPOILER
15-6621

48" FLEXIBLE FEED *

WINDOW TOP GUN
15-6620

MOUNT ASSY.
15-10412

STA
3F

STA
4

STA
5

STA
6

LEGEND

PART	MFGR.	MFGRS. NO.	B.A.C. INST. DWG.
A - ARMOR PLATE, TOP GUNNER	B. A. C.	3-15152	65-7387
B - ARMOR PLATE, TOP GUNNER	B. A. C.	3-15152-1	65-7387
C - ARMOR PLATE, TOP GUNNER	B. A. C.	6-10783	65-7387
D - ARMOR PLATE, BLKD. 4 DOOR	B. A. C.	6-10769	65-7387
E - UPPER TURRET GUN BREECH HEATERS (2) (A.C. SPEC. 24864 TYPE J-I L.H. & R.H.)*			55-7521
F - RADIO COMPARTMENT GUN BREECH HEATER (A.C. SPEC. 24864 TYPE J-I L.H.)*			15-10411
G - EJECTED SHELL BAG	B. A. C.	6-15203	15-10411
H - UPPER TURRET, POWER*	SPERRY GYROSCOPE CO.	645473E	55-7521
I - M-2, .50 CAL. MCH. GUN (2) (H39B5344)*			55-7521
J - RACK, BOMB (INBD.) (2)	B. A. C.	15-7954	15-7955
K - RACK, BOMB (OUTBD.) (2)	B. A. C.	15-7953	15-7955
L - HOIST FRAME, BOMB (STOWED)	B. A. C.	15-7582	15-7949
M - HANDLE, EMERGENCY BOMB RELEASE (41B10395)*			15-11194
N - MCH. GUN M-2, .50 CAL. (H39B5344) *	——	——	15-10411
O - SIGHT, GUN	B. A. C.	3-19578	15-10411
P - SIGHT, GUN	B. A. C.	3-19579	15-10411
Q - BOX, .50 CALIBER AMMUNITION	9.A.C.	14-3290	65-6806

* GOVERNMENT FURNISHED.

7-537

VIEW II-II

EXTERNAL BOMB
RACKS 15-9480
(SPECIAL EQUIPMENT)

Armament diagram from B-17 erection and maintenance manual shows snug fit for 2,000-pound bomb inside bay. Stowed position for radio compartment gun is indicated by dashed lines. (Carl Scholl/Aero Trader)

more fire retardant than the many twin-engine and even single-engine fire bombers in use. In 1960, the first of about two dozen Fortresses was modified with bomb bay tanks for dropping fire retardant.[4]

Along with surplus PB4Y-2 Privateers, the B-17s were the largest land-based fire bombers for many years until C-54s and DC-6s began making inroads. The legendary toughness of the Fortress, plus its honest flying traits, endeared it to civilian operators. Other Fortresses conducted large-area spraying, and a fleet of B-17s spread poison bait in a fire-ant abatement program in the southern United States in the 1960s.

When combat veteran B-17F 41-24485, the Memphis Belle, was unveiled in its domed facility in Memphis in May 1987, seven B-17s gathered for a flying tribute over the site. (Frederick A. Johnsen)

[1] Memo, "Account of the First Air Force Mission of the Korean War," by James A. Scheib, with attachment, "Aircraft Flight Report — Operations," 3rd Rescue Squadron, aircraft serial number 44-83885, 25 June 1950. [2] *Ibid.* [3] *Ibid.* [4] Peter M. Bowers, *Boeing Aircraft since 1916*, Naval Institute Press, Annapolis, Maryland, 1989.

SIGNIFICANT DATES

18 JUNE 1934
Boeing engineers began design of a four-engine bomber to meet an Air Corps specification.

28 JULY 1935
First flight of Boeing Model 299 prototype Flying Fortress.

30 OCTOBER 1935
Prototype Model 299 destroyed in crash at Wright Field.

2 DECEMBER 1936
First flight of a service-test Y1B-17 (number 36-149).

21 JULY 1940
First flight of B-17C.

8 JULY 1941
First Fortress combat mission flown by RAF with Fortress Is against German navy yard at Wilhelmshaven.

5 SEPTEMBER 1941
First flight of B-17E, first tailgun and power turret equipped Fortress.

17 AUGUST 1942
First Eighth Air Force B-17E mission against Rouen.

12 APRIL 1943
Board of officers including five from Eighth Air Force and one from the Royal Air Force completed the plan for the Combined Bomber Offensive (CBO) from the United Kingdom against Germany, under which the two services would coordinate attacks.

17 MAY 1943
Last (25th) combat mission for the B-17F Memphis Belle, before its return to the United States for war bond sales.

19 MAY 1943
First flight of XB-38, a B-17E converted by Lockheed-Vega to use Allison V-1710-89 liquid-cooled engines.

21 MAY 1943
First flight of B-17G.

1 NOVEMBER 1943
First 15th Air Force combat mission was a B-17 raid, attacking the La Spezia naval base and a railroad bridge at Vezzano.

FEBRUARY 1944
B-17s in natural metal finish began operations from England, contrasting with earlier camouflaged Fortresses.

4 MARCH 1944
First USAAF bombers over Berlin were B-17s from 95th and 100th bomb groups, dropping 67 tons.

24 APRIL 1944
First use of AZON (Azimuth Only) bomb by B-17 in Europe; 15th AF, with more tactical targets on its list than in the Eighth AF, tried AZON bombs which had radio device to permit bombardier to steer them in azimuth as they fell toward target. AZON had some utility against specific small targets like bridges.

9 APRIL 1945
Last Boeing-built Flying Fortress, B-17G-110-BO number 43-39508, rolled out of factory with ceremonies. It was delivered to the USAAF four days later — too late for combat.

13 JANUARY 1947
Air Force B-17G drone flown remotely, guided by another director B-17, from Eglin Field, Florida, to Washington, D.C., as a demonstration of capability.

14 OCTOBER 1959
Retirement of last U.S. Coast Guard PB-1G Fortress.

JUNE 1960
Last downing of a USAF target drone B-17.